BANNED

QUESTIONS ABOUT JESUS

QUESTIONS ABOUT JESUS

EDITED BY CHRISTIAN PIATT

CHALICE
PRESS

ST. LOUIS, MISSOURI

Bible quotations, unless otherwise noted, are from the New Revised Standard Version Bible, copyright 1989, Division of Christian Education of the National Council of the Churches of Christ in the United States of America. Used by permission. All rights reserved.

The opinions expressed in this work are those of the authors, and do not necessarily represent the opinions of the editors, the publisher, Chalice Press, Christian Board of Publication, or any associated persons or entities.

Cover image: iStockPhoto
Cover and interior design: Scribe Inc.

www.chalicepress.com

10 9 8 7 6 5 4 3 2 1   11 12 13 14 15 16

Print: 978-0-8272-02696   EPUB: 978-0-8272-02702   EPDF: 978-0-8272-02719

Library of Congress Cataloging–in–Publication Data

Banned questions about Jesus / edited by Christian Piatt.
   p. cm.
ISBN 978-0-8272-0269-6
   1. Jesus Christ—Miscellanea. I. Piatt, Christian. II. Title.
BT295.B25 2011
232—dc23   2011031370

Printed in United States of America

Contents

Contents

Contents

Contents

Introduction

Why a Book about Banned Questions?

When I was younger, I had a Bible thrown at my head during a Sunday school class for asking too many questions. Granted, I was probably even more provocative than your average adolescent, but I really did have a lot of legitimate questions about God, my faith, Jesus, and the Bible.

The message I got at the time was that church isn't the place for such questions.

Seriously? If we can't ask the tough, keep-you-awake-at-night questions within our faith communities, then what good are they?

I left organized religion behind for about ten years, until I found a place where my questions not only would be heard and tolerated but also would be respected and wrestled with. Beyond that, the good people at Chalice Press had either the nerve or the lack of judgment necessary to offer me a book series to help others struggling with these same questions.

In these pages you'll find fifty of the most provocative, challenging, or otherwise taboo questions that many of us have wondered about but few have actually asked. I assembled an incredible team of respondents to offer their views on these hard questions. Their responses range from the personal to the profound and from sarcastic to deeply touching. I'm deeply grateful to each of them and for their commitment to sharing their hearts, minds, and experiences.

The goal of this book is not to resolve these difficult issues once and for all but rather to open up an ongoing dialogue that allows us all to talk more openly together about what we believe and what we don't and, perhaps more importantly, why we believe it.

I strongly believe that any faith worth claiming should stand up to rigorous examination and should also be open to change over time. I hope that this collection is one step in your continuing journey as a person of faith, whatever that may look like to you.

If you enjoy this book, be sure to check out *Banned Questions about the Bible*, the first book in the *Banned Questions* series. And if you have questions you'd like me to consider for future editions or if you think of a topic for another *Banned Questions* book, write me at cpiatt@christianpiatt.com and tell me about it.

Christian

1. Why would God send Jesus as the sacrificial lamb of God, dying for the sins of the world, instead of just destroying sin or perhaps offering grace and forgiveness to the very ones created by God? Why does an all-powerful being need a mediator anyway?

Chris Haw

Who is...
Chris Haw

I apparently grind my teeth at night, perhaps in anticipation of my eternal destiny.

I have found it important for my mind to get the "sacrificial lamb" idea back into working shape by, for example, considering how Jesus also died *from the sins of the world*. A terrible steamroller of mob violence, groupthink, and sacred violence struck down Jesus—as it struck down many others. A multitude of our sins, not God, killed Jesus. What is hopeful, however, is how he did not squirm under the temptations to violate love (even toward his enemy) and reduce himself to the level of his torturers and accusers. This fortuitous and righteous display of love is not tangential to his mission—for *God is love*. This witness is salvific not only because it is a good example to live by—which it is—but also because it is *now part of the human story*. Humanity has a chance—for at least *one* of its members lived in truth.

As to a "mediator" this seems (at least) like a confusion of words: Forgiveness needs mediation like a sentence needs words. When I forgive you for stealing my couch, I need the mediation of an action or a word to make my forgiveness real—or else it is mere sentiment in my mind. But to go even further beyond a mediated forgiveness, and enter into truth and reconciliation, you are going to need to also return my couch! Is that not how the metaphor of the "Word of God made flesh" works? We need at least one human not only to receive God's mercy—which has been latent in the universe since before it began—but also to return God's couch, so to speak; Jesus, the tradition seems to say, is the human to have done so.

And for what it is worth, the "sending his son" verse should not be understood as God killing someone. (Did God's denunciation of human sacrifice not begin with the binding of Isaac?) No, *We* killed God's Son, and it was sinful and unjust; Jesus' freely accepting his (pseudolegal) mob scapegoating does not legitimize it but instead attempts to overcome it with love. Thus John 3:16–21 should be understood constructively as God sending us righteousness incarnate—the way of true love in visible expression—not a great person to torture and satiate a bloodlust.

Lee C. Camp

Who is...
Lee C. Camp

I like playing the upright bass.

A. There is a long and complex tradition of varying interpretations of the meaning of the death of Jesus. The early church primarily thought of the death of Jesus as a victory over the powers of sin and death. Sin was not understood merely as the willful act of breaking God's rules, but as a power that enslaved and corrupted God's good creation. Personified in Satan, that power was always pulling humans down to the grave, punishment, and wrath. In Jesus, God overcame the rebellious powers through suffering love.

In the medieval era, another trajectory became predominant in the West. Anselm of Canterbury argued that a God-man was necessitated because of the great gravity of sin: Sin dishonored God, and humankind had to make some reparation, some *satisfaction* for sin. Humankind was unable to make such a repayment, and thus Jesus became the substitute, restoring the honor due to God through his obedience unto death. By the sixteenth century, John Calvin focused on *punishment*: Because of the immensity of humankind's sin, God's wrath demanded punishment. Jesus became the substitute punishment.

Peter Abelard, a contemporary with Anselm, argued that it was neither reparation nor punishment that God demanded, but repentance. Thus the loving example of Jesus effects a change in the heart of humankind, bringing about such repentance.

There has been renewed attention to this doctrine in the last number of decades: Numerous interpreters are assessing the variety in the Christian tradition not as mutually exclusive and competing interpretations but as metaphors—each having its own particular strengths and weaknesses—that give us different glimpses of the profound historical fact of a crucified Messiah.

Jarrod McKenna

Who is...
Jarrod McKenna

I think Žižek is right in insisting trivial "interesting facts" about the author function as a form of propaganda to show we are "balanced," that is, "he's not just a crazy activist he also likes Scrabble and long walks on the beach."

Ever read Leviticus 16? Odd text. Yet French anthropologist René Girard reminds us that, despite how primitive Leviticus 16 might seem to us, every culture creates "scapegoats."

Scapegoats are those we blame to keep us in the dark to what has shaped us, namely, the systems that demand victims. Nero put early Christians to the stake. Europe burnt powerful women as witches. Magisterial reformers drowned the Anabaptists. Colonizers deliberately infected indigenous peoples with smallpox. Nazis took millions of Jews to the gas chambers. Jim Crow America lynched black America. The Australian government imprisons "boat people" seeking refuge. A Christian school fires a teacher because of her sexual orientation despite her passion for Jesus. To maintain their place in the "cool group," kids universally seek out and identify "geeks." Guantanamo tortures innocents, fearing they are terrorists. All this is done to keep us "safe," to maintain "order," to protect "us," and restore "peace." In the face of this reality, *our* reality, "total depravity" seems optimistic.

The gospel is not that some deity takes out its rage on an innocent victim so he doesn't have to take it out on all of us eternally. This is a diabolical lie dressed up in Christian drag that reverses the gospel, making it the same old bad news, while concealing that Jesus is victorious over it. God doesn't need blood. God doesn't need a mediator. *We do!*

In Jesus, God knowingly becomes the scapegoat, as "the Lamb of God who takes away the sins of the world" (John 1:29). The lamb of God is NOT offered *to* God by humanity but *is God* offered to us to enable a new humanity. God is reconciling the world to Godself through Christ by knowingly becoming our victim, exposing this idolatrous system that promises order, safety, peace, and protection in exchange for victims. In the resurrection, we are all confronted with the grace of our Creator in the forgiving victim who sends the Holy Spirit to shape a new world where no more blood needs to be shed.

Christian Piatt

A. The two-dollar phrase for the concept raised in this question is "substitutionary atonement" or "blood atonement." The idea that the sacrifice of a living creature was required to appease God for one's sins has been around for a lot longer than Christianity has. Mentions of animal sacrifice can be found throughout the Old Testament, and Abraham's faith is even tested when he's asked to sacrifice his own son.

This value of sacrifice as part of one's faith was also common in the Roman culture, in which the types of sacrifices usually were specific to the characteristics of the gods being worshipped. So a god of the harvest would require an offering of produce, and so on. Some pre-Christian cultures, such as those from Carthage, even practiced human sacrifice, though the Romans generally condemned it.

In the fourth century C.E., Gregory of Nyssa proposed that Jesus' death was an act of liberation, freeing humanity from enslavement to Satan. Seven hundred years later, Anselm developed what was then known as the "satisfaction" concept, which is closest to what we think of now as atonement theology. Jesus, being both human and perfectly divine, was the only sacrifice that could appease the offense to God by human sin. This idea pointed to Romans and Galatians as support for this interpretation.

Around the same time, a theologian named Peter Abelard proposed that it actually was Jesus' response of pure—some might emphasize *nonviolent*—love in the face of violence, hatred, and death that was transformative in the human psyche, reorienting us toward a theology of sacrificial love over justice or atonement. Walter Wink has gone a step further and claimed that atonement theology is a corruption of the gospel, focusing on an act of violence rather than the values of peaceful humility and compassion lived and taught by Christ.

Pablo A. Jiménez

Who is...
Pablo A. Jiménez

I am a Latin percussionist.

A. Metaphors, metaphors; religious language is poetic. Given that God is "Other," we can hardly understand who God is. Therefore, we use metaphorical language in order to convey our ideas about God. This language is always contextual. This means that we usually compare

God to things we know, particularly to creation. In theology, this is called the *analogia entis*, a Latin phrase, which means the "analogy of being."

Therefore, it should not surprise us that ancient religious language is based on metaphors. The question addresses three common metaphors. The first is an agricultural one, in which Jesus is compared to a lamb that is sacrificed for the benefit of the community. The second is a legal metaphor that compares the sinner with people condemned to death for their crimes. The third is a political image, which describes Jesus as the mediator between the people and God, the powerful King.

Every generation has the responsibility of rethinking the faith, searching for new and more effective metaphors to describe the relationship between God and humanity. However, before tossing out the old metaphors, we need to understand their meaning. In a way, theology is a dialogue across generations, time, and space. Before developing our own theological language, we must try to understand what other generations said about God, Jesus, and other common theological themes.

Amy Reeder Worley

Who is...
Amy Reeder Worley

I am from Mount Sterling, Kentucky, the home of Mt. Sterling Court Days, a festival where a person can buy a gun, ammo, tube socks, black market CDs, and corndogs, all within one mile of the courthouse.

The idea that Jesus died as the "sacrificial lamb of God" is called "substitutionary atonement," which is a fancy way of saying that Jesus was crucified as a sacrifice to pay the "sin debt" of humanity. Although for many Christians atonement is essential to Christianity, it wasn't articulated fully until a thousand years *after* Jesus' death in a treatise by Anselm of Canterbury. Regrettably, many people are unaware of a body of biblical scholarship skeptical of substitutionary atonement.

When trying to glean meaning from sacred texts, it helps to consider whatever knowledge we have about the writer, his political and social world, and to whom he wrote. For example, some cite Paul's letters as supporting substitutionary atonement. However, when we read Paul in context, we understand two important things. First, Paul wrote to early Christians during the first century C.E., long before Anselm's exposition on atonement. Second,

Paul was a practicing Jew during a time in Jewish history when believers sacrificed animals at the Temple, seeking forgiveness for violations of the law.

Given his religious heritage, it is unsurprising that Paul borrowed from the Jewish tradition of sacrificial atonement. The use of atonement-related language does not necessarily mean, however, that Paul thought Jesus was literally a sacrificial lamb for humankind.

I would argue that substitutionary atonement is logically inconsistent with Paul's writing about a loving and compassionate God who freely bestows grace on the world. Reading Paul as a Jew writing under Roman imperial rule, we can see him trying to teach early Christians about *the interrelation* of Jesus' crucifixion *and* resurrection.

Rome executed Jesus in part because of his radically antiestablishment message, and because some believed he sought political power. I believe that Jesus was crucified *because of human sin, not in the place of humans who sin.* Because of the resurrection, Jesus (and his followers) ultimately defeats death and arises victorious.

Paul summarized this view of Jesus' death and resurrection when he urged early Christians to "die" to sin and "live again in" Christ.

Scriptural References

Leviticus 16; Mark 10:35–45; Luke 11:49–51; John 10:33; Romans 3:24–25; 6:19–23; 12:2; 1 Corinthians 1:17—2:16; 2 Corinthians 5:18–21; Galatians 3: 1–14; Hebrews 10:10

Suggested Additional Sources for Reading

- James Alison, *Knowing Jesus* (Templegate, 1994).
- James Alison, *The Joy of Being Wrong* (Crossroad, 1998).
- René Girard, *I See Satan Fall Like Lightning* (Orbis, 1991).
- Karen Armstrong, *The Battle for God* (Ballantine, 2001).
- Gustaf Aulen, *Christus Victor* (Macmillan, 1931).
- Marcus Borg, *Jesus: Uncovering the Life, Teachings, and Relevance of a Religious Revolutionary* (HarperSanFrancisco, 2006).
- Marcus Borg and John Crossan, *The First Paul: Reclaiming the Radical Visionary Behind the Church's Conservative Icon* (HarperOne, 2009).
- Walter Wink, *Jesus and Nonviolence: A Third Way* (Fortress Press, 2003).
- Walter Wink, *The Powers That Be: Theology for a New Millennium* (Doubleday, 1998).
- Paul Tillich, *Systematic Theology*, vol. 2 (Univ. of Chicago Press, 1957).
- Joel B. Green and Mark D. Baker, *Recovering the Scandal of the Cross: Atonement in the New Testament and Contemporary Contexts* (InterVarsity, 2000).

- James Wm. McClendon Jr., "The Saving Cross: Atonement" in *Systematic Theology*, vol. 2, *Doctrine* (Abingdon Press, 1994).
- Brad Jersak and Michael Hardin, *Stricken by God?: Nonviolent Identification and the Victory of Christ* (Eerdmans, 2007).

Suggested Questions for Further Discussion/Thought

1. What stories have you heard preachers tell to explain the meaning of Jesus' crucifixion? Which one of the traditions of interpretation does that story illustrate?
2. Does this view of the crucifixion challenge your faith?
3. Does it lend more or less credibility to the Christian faith?
4. Does it make Jesus' death any less relevant to Christianity?
5. Were you raised with the idea that Jesus died for your sins? How has this influenced your understanding of the Christian faith?
6. Do you believe that God would condone sacrificing a man in payment for the sins of the world? Why or why not?
7. Have you encountered arguments against, or alternatives to, atonement theology? What do you think of them?

Question

2. Many Christians embrace the phrase, "I believe Jesus is the Christ, the son of the living God, and I accept him as my personal Lord and Savior," but I can't find this anywhere in the Bible. Where did it come from?

Amy Reeder Worley

Who is...
Amy Reeder Worley

My ex-fiancé introduced me to my husband—no it wasn't like that.

A. I sometimes dream those words—a refrain carved in my memory. I'm haunted by the voice of my congregation repeating the gospel hymn "Just as I Am" until someone went to the altar to pray. My pastor's hands and voice were high as he demanded, "Have YOU accepted Jesus Christ as YOUR personal Lord and Savior? Have YOU asked the Lord's forgiveness and become a Christian?"

As a girl, I was taught that the Bible said, without any other possible interpretation, there is one God, one faith, one baptism, and one way to God the Father via his son Jesus Christ, who died on the cross *because of my sins*. Those who did not have a "personal relationship" with Jesus were not saved. Not saved meant being doomed to hell.

I ultimately had to leave the church for years to exorcise this theology. And I still haven't completely lost the involuntary guilt it left in me. Those words, putting Jesus' death and the state of my soul in my small hands, are etched in my cells, leaving me somehow a bit wounded.

The distressing part of this message is that it puts all of Christianity on the Christian. It is graceless. The emphasis on a "personal" relationship with Jesus implies that salvation is somehow entirely self-initiated.

I don't believe that was Jesus' message. Jesus said that no one gets to the Father but through him. But he also said to follow him because he was *of* God and *knew* God. Jesus spoke of God's unconditional love, which is available to all who are open to receive it. God's love is not ours personally; it's communal. Jesus spoke about the kingdom of God and there cannot be a kingdom of one.

I have an Anne Lamott quote on my computer that sums it up for me. She says, "I do not at all understand the mystery of grace—only that it meets us where we are but does not leave us where it found us." God comes to us, not

9

just "I," but "us"—all of us. That is the very nature of grace. Our relationship with God is by its very nature not personal but collective.

Chris Haw

Who is...
Chris Haw

I played in punk rock bands in high school.

The phrase comes from a conglomeration of excerpts from the book of Romans, Peter's confession in Mark, and a few other places. But nowhere does the modifier "personal Lord" makes it into the New Testament as this is a misnomer: "Lords" are by their nature public and political beings. More important, as many scholars are now admitting, to call Jesus your "Lord and Savior" in the first century is to say, "Caesar is not."

The phrase invites (nearly sarcastic) political provocation and paradox through the exaltation of the humiliated and crucified "Lord." The phrase means, I exalt the humbled, or I give power to the powerless one, or I favor the unfavored, or I love the unloved, and so on.

Jarrod McKenna

The "Sinners' Prayer" is not in the Bible. Variations of it arose in the Great Awakenings, when evangelists were helping people make faith personal. God is gracious and will work with anything, but there is a very real danger today in our hyperindividualistic cultures that the Sinners' Prayer can become a magic incantation to avoid hell rather than something that helps us live as a prayer in response to the grace God has shown us.

The early Christians did not pray the Sinners' Prayer as isolated individuals to become Christians. They prayed the Lord's Prayer as communities in response to the grace of God. They responded to the gospel by becoming part of such a people by entering into the waters of baptism. More than just a personal prayer, baptism was a political changing of allegiances, facilitating the death of the nationalism, patriotism, racism, violence, lust, and greed that named us. Through baptism, the early Christians were raised in the name of the Triune God (Matthew 28:19, Galatians 3:26–29) to walk as Jesus walked (1 John 2:6) and were immersed in the narrative of God's liberating work throughout history, of which Christ is the culmination. They were immersed in the reality of the repentance, forgiveness of sins, and the gift of the Holy Spirit of God's future (Acts 2:38), birthed anew into God's New World breaking in (John 3:3–5, 1 Peter 1:3, Titus 3:5). They died to their old selves, formed in the patterns of the kingdoms of this world, and were raised with Christ into the nonviolent redemptive patterns of discipleship (Romans 6:3–11, Colossians 2:12).

In doing so they didn't merely invite Jesus into their heart as their personal Lord and Savior. More than that, they responded to Jesus' invitation to enter into God's heart to heal all of creation. It was not merely an outward sign of an inner reality; it was a personal appropriation of the outward coming of the kingdom of God. They pledged allegiance to Christ as cosmic Lord and Savior of all creation (1 Peter 3:21). As evangelists, we are commissioned to invite the world to pray the Lord's Prayer with us as we witness to the kingdom coming on earth (Matthew 6:9–13).

R. M. Keelan Downton

A. While I've never heard it in that particular form, the first part comes from an exchange between Peter and Jesus recorded in the gospel of Matthew. Jesus first asks what other people are saying about him and then asks, *but who do you say I am?* The significance of Jesus as personal savior is more the product of nineteenth- and twentieth-century reflection of certain parts of the church. The adjective "personal" was used to distinguish those seeking to cultivate spiritual life through intentional practices (the *method* of Methodism, though they were not the only ones to do so) from the impersonal deist god of the enlightenment that motivated so many of the "founding fathers" of the United States.

It later came to interact with the hyperindividualism of liberal democratic capitalism to make encounters with God another commoditized expression of identity, like jeans or a cell phone case (also the source of "worship" songs that leave the uninitiated unsure whether you are referring to Jesus or a girlfriend).

There is something important in the idea that Jesus came for *me*, but in a culture that's already so focused on "me," we probably need a little more focus on Jesus as the Messiah or Christ who came to challenge the apparent order of the world and invite us to join in the process of revealing the true order of the world by proclaiming and embodying it.

Scriptural References

Matthew 6:9–13; 28:19; John 3:3–5; Acts 2:38; Romans 6:3–11; Galatians 3:26–29; Colossians 2:12; Titus 3:5; 1 Peter 1:3; 3:21; 1 John 2:6

Suggested Additional Sources for Reading

- Henry Nouwen, *The Return of the Prodigal Son* (Continuum, 1995).
- Anne Lamott, *Grace Eventually, Thoughts on Faith* (Riverhead, 2007).
- George Lindbeck, *The Nature of Doctrine: Religion and Theology in a Postliberal Age* (Westminster, 1984).
- Susan Campbell, *Dating Jesus: A Story of Fundamentalism, Feminism, and the American Girl* (Beacon, 2009).
- Fredrick Buechner, *The Alphabet of Grace* (Harper & Row, 1970).
- Margaret Atwood, *The Handmaid's Tale* (McLelland & Stewart, 1985).
- Gregory A. Boyd, *The Myth of a Christian Religion* (Zondervan, 2009).
- Lee Camp, *Mere Discipleship* (Brazos Press, 2003).
- John H. Yoder, *Body Politics* (Discipleship Resources, 1992).
- N. T. Wright, *Jesus and the Victory of God* (Augsburg Fortress Press, 1997).

Suggested Questions for Further Discussion/Thought

1. Do you believe faith is personal or communal?
2. Amy's piece speaks about being wounded by a theological message. Have you ever experienced that? Is healing possible?
3. What do you understand about grace? Can we ever "deserve" it?
4. What does it say about God if salvation is only available to those who accept church dogma?
5. What if instead of inviting people to pray the Sinners' Prayer, we invited them to pray the Lord's Prayer and to explore what emersion into God's New World might mean for them? How would this change the way we share the gospel?

3. In John 14:6, Jesus says, "I am the way, and the truth, and the life. No one comes to the Father except through me." Do people have to choose to follow Jesus to go to heaven? And what does it mean to choose his way?

Phil Snider

A lot of people think this verse means that only those who accept Jesus into their heart as their personal Lord and Savior will go to heaven. But if you read the gospels closely, you'll see that Jesus never mentions this as a requirement for salvation. I tend to think that faith in Jesus should make us more inclusive of others rather than less. While people are quite good at building walls of exclusion, it's the upside-down kingdom of God announced by Jesus that knocks them down time and again, precisely because Jesus' way—in stark contrast to our own—is "the truth, and the life." Accordingly, heaven can be viewed as that place and time (no matter which side of the grave you happen to be on) in which God's love reigns supreme.

Furthermore, I don't think that choosing Christ is a one-time affair, but rather a decision I make (or don't make) every moment of my life. As Peter Rollins suggests, I choose Christ's way "when I stand up for those who are forced to live on their knees, when I speak for those who have had their tongues torn out, when I cry for those who have no more tears left to shed,"[1] *yet I deny Christ every time I don't.* So you might say I'm aspiring to be a Christian, and in the best moments of my life, as few and as far between as they are, I hope to become one.

Chris Haw

John's mysterious gospel also mentions that no one can "choose Jesus" except by being drawn by the Father. Perhaps one might think that John was anachronistically agreeing with Calvinism's predestination or Augustinianism.

I think it is best to interpret John's point in light of the larger scope of his theology. The best way to interpret this verse is to understand what Jesus is to John: Jesus has God's full life in him. And that life is *love*—for "God is love."

Simply, if you do not have the life of God in you, you cannot go on living after your biological life gives way. This isn't a matter of exclusion; it is a way

---

1. Peter Rollins, "My Confession: I Deny the Resurrection," accessed April 29, 2010, http://peterrollins.net/?p=136.

of identifying the principle by which life persists: God's being, which is love. Admittedly this position, intermingled as it is with the resurrection of the dead, appears to us as extremely optimistic—that love animates life.

In popular imagery, we have retained this thought by symbolizing the heart with love—not an obvious connection when you think about it. Perhaps even more interestingly, we have some biological findings that should give us pause when we declare our modern veto on all miracles and our ban on the resurrection: "At the organismal level, there are no physiological or thermo-dynamic reasons why death must occur. In fact, there are several unicellular species that are immortal and one advanced multicellular organism that has not demonstrated any signs of senescence (Bristlecone Pine)."[2]

So from a certain perspective, "choosing Jesus" means choosing life, which means choosing love. But love is a profoundly confused term and begs not only a definition but also a specific example. Jesus is apparently our most excellent example of love. Therefore, if you reject him, you are rejecting love. I appreciate how the church has maintained a canon of saints to clarify other echoes of Jesus, so we keep our minds tuned to what "accepting Jesus" looks like.

Peter J. Walker

Who is...
Peter J. Walker

My wife let me change our wedding date so I could enroll in a seminary class taught by Brian McLaren.

Historically, Christianity has taught a fairly exclusive doctrine of salvation: Those who don't accept Christ are condemned to hell. That teaching is easier to accept when you are (a) an oppressed believer, living under violent persecution or (b) part of a theocratic society where *everyone* is Christian. In either scenario, it's unlikely that typical Christians faced the dilemma of a neighbor or loved one who did not believe. That's probably a core reason our soteriology (study of religious doctrines of salvation) developed and cemented as it did. In the twenty-first century, however, we confront this problem daily with friends, family, coworkers, and classmates.

---

2. Jeffrey Schloss, "From Evolution to Eschatology," in *Resurrection: Theological and Scientific Assessments*, ed. Ted Peters, Robert John Russell, and Michael Welker (Grand Rapids, MI: Eerdmans, 2002), 83; see also Stuart Kauffman, *The Origins of Order* (Oxford: Oxford University, 1993).

There are plenty of scriptures available for constructing arguments in favor of exclusivism, inclusivism, and universalism. No one "wins" that fight. We all choose to believe what seems true to us. Many of the most conservative Christians I have known still make special allowances for people they care about—people who "couldn't possibly go to hell!"

Objective truth is one thing; subjective relationships are another. My friend Jim Henderson (http://www.offthemap.com) says, "When people like each other, the rules change." Many of these changed rules remain secret because people are scared of risking judgment or reproach from their churches. I have decided to accept the backlash and make my rule breaking public because I think it's helpful to talk about these things openly.

I know that my salvation is in Christ, but I don't demand that of others. If Jesus came only to offer exclusive salvation through himself, then he actually made things worse for folks, not better. I believe Jesus flung the door to God wide open! George Fox, the founder of Quakerism, referred to an "inner light" that every human being carries: God's immediate presence. I affirm that spiritual connection in us all, and believe it is inherently salvific.

Sherri Emmons

Who is...
Sherri Emmons

I tend to take in strays—dogs, cats, birds, and sometimes people.

A. This is one of the hardest passages in the New Testament for me, because it seems to run counter to so many of Jesus' other teachings about compassion and forgiveness. I have a hard time imagining a God who would turn away people because they didn't follow a particular way or didn't even know about that way.

If we take seriously the image of God as a father, then we have to believe God loves his children. As a mother, I cannot imagine any sin so horrific that I would condemn my children to everlasting damnation. Surely God is not a worse parent than I am.

A friend shared a metaphor about heaven that makes a lot of sense to me. We are all climbing a mountain toward the kingdom of God, and there are many different paths we can follow. Not all of them reach the top. Some lead to dead ends. Some lead to disaster. But I believe there is more than one path to the top. And Jesus himself gave us a road map when he said, "Thus you will know them by their fruits" (Matthew 7:20).

Do people have to choose to follow Jesus to go to heaven?

Amy Reeder Worley

Who is...
Amy Reeder Worley

I was the first runner up in the Montgomery County Junior Miss Pageant. Sadly, the Junior Miss was able to fulfill her duties.

A. John is the newest and most unique of the gospels. Although none of the gospels were written as purely historical accounts of the life and times of Jesus, John is the most mythical (truth revealed through the totality of a narrative rather than a logical theorem) and mystical (the pursuit of union with the Divine).

Because John differs from the synoptics (Matthew, Mark, and Luke) in its Christology and language, there is substantial scholarly disagreement about its ultimate message. However, most scholars agree that the author of John's view of Jesus is revelatory—Jesus came to reveal the path to God. In John, Jesus claims to be "the bread of life" (6:35), "the light of the world" (8:12), "the Advocate" (or "paraclete") (14:16), and "the life" (14:6). This metaphorical language evokes images of Jesus feeding the spiritually hungry, lighting the path for those who cannot see it, and drawing our attention to the sacred around us.

We should note that Jesus does not say, "no one gets to *heaven* but through me." Rather, he refers to getting to the Father. This is in keeping with John's somewhat mystical theology concerning the human experience of God. Second, although the second sentence of John 14:6 asserts the exclusivity of Jesus as the path to God, the first sentence explains *why* Jesus is the "way" to God. Jesus is the" truth," meaning his message was true. Jesus is the "life," meaning his life was a map to experience God. In other words according to John's gospel, Jesus embodied the way to God.

So is Jesus the *only* way to God? I don't think so. John was written during a time when the early Christian church sought legitimacy. It was distinguishing itself from Judaism and the Roman cults. I like to view the exclusive language in John 14:6 as an emphatic affirmation of the truth in Jesus' message, not a condemnation of other paths to God.

Scriptural References

John 6:35; 8:12; 14:6; 14:16; Romans 5:18; Philippians 2:10–11; 1 Timothy 4:10

Suggested Additional Sources for Reading

- Douglas John Hall, *Why Christian? For Those on the Edge of Faith* (Fortress Press, 1998).
- Danielle Shroyer, *The Boundary-Breaking God: An Unfolding Story of Hope and Promise* (Jossey-Bass, 2009).
- Peter Rollins, *The Orthodox Heretic* (Paraclete Press, 2009).
- Eric Stetson, *Christian Universalism: God's Good News for All People* (Sparkling Bay, 2008).
- H. Larry Ingle, *First among Friends: George Fox and the Creation of Quakerism* (Oxford Univ. Press, 1994).
- Marcus J. Borg, *The Heart of Christianity: Rediscovering a Life of Faith* (HarperSanFrancisco, 2003).
- The Christian Universalist Association: http://www.christianuniversalist.org.
- Philip Gulley and James Mulholland, *If Grace Is True: Why God Will Save Every Person* (HarperSanFrancisco, 2003).

Suggested Questions for Further Discussion/Thought

1. If you affirm faith in Jesus Christ as God's representative, does that make you more or less inclusive of others?
2. Do you believe that God's love transcends doctrines, creeds, and religions? If so, how does that affect the way you view non-Christian religions? Does such a perspective diminish God's love or expand God's love?
3. Is it possible to be on Christ's way even if you don't believe in God? Is it possible to be transformed by God if you don't believe in God?
4. When we talk about heaven what do you think most people mean?
5. What about Jesus made him "the way, and the truth, and the life"?
6. How does John's Jesus differ from the Jesus of the synoptics?
7. Does a religion need to be *exclusively* true to be true?

4. Did Jesus ever have sex? Did he have sexual fantasies and desires?

L. Shannon Moore

Who is...
L. Shannon Moore

My favorite words (in order) are cloak, jolly, and goblin.

I doubt that Jesus ever had sex. First off, even though he liked to rock the boat with religious leaders, Jesus was a devout Jew—he knew the scriptures and laws well. Adultery (when you're married and have sex with somebody else) is clearly off limits. It even made God's "Top Ten List of Sins." And while most of the other laws regarding sexual conduct deal with cleanliness and not doing it with relatives, they don't come right out and say, "You can't have sex before you get married." Yet the wording of these laws implies that, in that culture, sex and marriage go together. The book of Deuteronomy mandates that a rapist marry his victim, for goodness' sake.

Jesus himself says that lusting after a woman in your heart is just as bad as adultery—since I'm gay, I don't have to worry about that one—and criticizes one woman for living with a man who isn't her husband. So since the Bible does not indicate whether he was ever married, I'm thinking our Lord kept his virginity.

As for sexual fantasies, I'm going with a big yes on that one. I don't think Jesus would have been fully human if he hadn't had sexual desires. However, he didn't want us to be controlled by sexual thoughts or to view others as objects for our own selfish desires.

I wouldn't rule out the possibility of his having wet dreams, though it would make me kind of jealous to know that he did, since they've always seemed to elude me.

Becky Garrison

Who is...
Becky Garrison

Since 1996, I've been studying improv theater with Gary Austin, founder of the Groundlings.

A. While the sex life of Jesus and the disciples never comes up in the New Testament, Jesus does talk about the need for marital fidelity and cautions against having sex outside of a committed relationship. Given that there's no mention of Jesus being betrothed to a woman, it's a pretty safe bet he died a virgin.

But since Jesus was fully divine and fully human, that means he faced all the temptations and urges that we mere mortals deal with on a daily basis. So using that logic, then yes, Jesus would have gotten erections replete with wet dreams. However, because he was fully divine, he was able to keep these urges more under control than us.

Also, as a classy dude who was also a rabbi, he knew it would be not only unclean but tacky to tell even his disciples about any sexual fantasies he might have had.

Tripp Fuller

Who is...
Tripp Fuller

I love Shaq.

A. Despite the conspiracy theories of a Jesus and Mary Magdalene love affair, historians are hard pressed to answer a question about Jesus actually having sex. Any answer would have to be extrapolated from personal or theological convictions due to historical silence. More important here is the question of typical psychological and biological expressions of a healthy man. We can say much more about these questions because as Christians we affirm the full humanity of Jesus and stand on this side of the scientific revolution.

Jesus' brain, like all human brains, is biologically the product of millions of years of evolutionary development. To be human is to have a brain that includes a reptilian component focusing with intensity on safety, food, and

19

sex. Of course there are more complex parts, including the frontal cortex with which humans are able make commitments, but clearly we would not be here as a species if we were not more successful than our competition at getting food and not dying before reproducing. So when it comes to wrestling with questions of sex, it is best just to admit that we not only occasionally have sex on the brain but sex is hardwired in our brains!

Did a fully human Jesus have, as part of his brain, a piece that quite naturally wants to turn females into objects of DNA replication? Yes. But what did he do with the "reptile" in the head? In the Sermon on the Mount, Jesus says, "You have heard that it was said, 'You shall not commit adultery.' But I say to you that everyone who looks at a woman with lust has already committed adultery with her in his heart" (Matthew 5:27–28).

Here Jesus affirms that one shouldn't engage in the act of adultery, but more than that he calls us to not look at a woman lustfully, as an object, or—you could say—"with our inner reptile." The force of Jesus' statement should lead us to think through these questions about sex, seeking to keep people as subjects to whom we relate rather than as objects of selfish desire. That is something I think Jesus did as part of his complete faithfulness to God.

Scriptural References

Exodus 20:14; Leviticus 18; Deuteronomy 22:28–29; Matthew 5:27–28; Mark 10:1–12; John 4:16–18

Suggested Additional Sources for Reading

- Nikos Kazantzakis, trans. P. A. Bien, *The Last Temptation of Christ* (Simon and Schuster, 1960).
- Martin Scorsese, director, *The Last Temptation of Christ* (Universal Films, 1988).

Suggested Questions for Further Discussion/Thought

1. Shannon says, "*In that culture*, sex and marriage go together." Does culture have anything to do with sexual values?
2. Do you think it is OK to have sex before marriage? Why or why not?
3. How do you feel about depictions of Jesus in movies like *The Last Temptation of Christ* that deal with Jesus' humanity, including his sexuality?

5. Why did Jesus have to suffer so much before he died? Or did he have to?

David Lose

Who is...
David Lose

I own enough Norwegian sweaters to wear a different one every day of the week—and I'm not even a little bit Norwegian.

How you answer this question says a lot about how you understand God. Most people who believe Jesus "had" to suffer understand God primarily in terms of God's justice. Jesus "had" to suffer and die because he is taking our deserved punishment. Because God's justice has been offended by human sin, some kind of punishment or restitution must be made or God's justice itself is mocked. Because Jesus is fully human, he can stand in for us; because he is fully God, his suffering counts as payment for all of us. It's a clear, neat, and eminently logical theory. But I hate it. Notice: God can't forgive us until payment is made, until blood is shed. God's justice trumps God's love.

So what if Jesus didn't "have" to suffer? Instead, what if Jesus suffered because the love and forgiveness he offered was just too incomprehensible and terrifying for us to accept. Forgiveness is terrifying because it assumes guilt, brokenness, and the need for forgiveness. No wonder the sinners and tax collectors loved listening to Jesus—they already knew they were down and out (Luke 15:1). And no wonder the scribes and Pharisees wanted him dead—he offended their sense of self-sufficiency as much as their sense of self-righteousness (Luke 15:2, John 3:16–21).

From this point of view, Jesus didn't "have to" suffer and die, but he did so anyway in order to show us just how much God loves us. He suffered because he proclaimed God's mercy, love, and forgiveness, and until you've lost everything, there's nothing more terrifying to hear.

21

Mark Van Steenwyk

Who is...
Mark Van Steenwyk

I honestly believe that Buffy the Vampire Slayer *was one of the best television shows ever.*

Jesus was executed through the particularly brutal process of crucifixion. Before that, he was whipped and beaten and psychologically traumatized. Did he *really* need to go through all that before he died? Well, it depends.

If you're asking if we would be less forgiven for our sins if Jesus had been killed by a more "humane" method like a quick beheading then no. Torture wasn't some sort of prerequisite for forgiveness. Some folks like to argue that Jesus needed to suffer more than any other person in order to be an acceptable sacrifice to cover over our sins. I absolutely disagree.

However, I think Jesus *did* have to suffer as much as he did. Why? Because Jesus was profoundly committed to being in solidarity with those who suffer oppression. He was willing to embrace the worst that the authorities could throw at him without being broken. He was willing to be treated as the worst sort of criminal. He was willing to be treated as less than human because he himself recognized the humanity of all.

When a prisoner is treated like trash, Jesus understands. When a beggar is spat upon, Jesus understands. When someone is victimized, marginalized, or dehumanized because of their gender, age, race, beliefs, ethnic group or political affiliation, income level, or occupation, Jesus understands. He was—and is—in solidarity with the oppressed. That is why he suffered so much: because he loves so much.

Peter J. Walker

Who is...
Peter J. Walker

I once went out on a homosexual date—accidentally!

Typically the Christian economics of sin and forgiveness demand a price for humanity's wickedness. There are lots of theories as to how this works: Jesus paid our ransom, took our punishment, and so on, but they all generally agree that sin creates a vacuum in the universe that must be filled.

Jesus Christ's mission on earth undermined all the conventional wisdom of justice, salvation, power, and hierarchy that the world so naturally accumulates. It was gentle and counterintuitive, and it frustrated the motives of selfishness, ambition, and dominance. Jesus told people what was true, not what they wanted to hear. At first they interpreted it the way they wanted to and dreamed of a new Davidic kingdom. When they realized Jesus wasn't going to deliver what they envisioned, they turned on him. Broken, scared, selfish people did what broken, scared, selfish people tend to do: They ravaged and brutalized what was pure.

The miracle of Jesus is the portrayal of a God who suffers: a weak and dying God, who chooses to identify with humanity firsthand.

Did Jesus *have to* suffer and die? I don't think God demanded it. Was it an inevitability given the innate conflict between darkness and light? Absolutely. In that way, I agree that sin creates a vacuum in the universe: It is inherent dysfunction. In the natural order, actions have equal, opposite reactions. In the supernatural order, Jesus Christ's interruption into history created an overcompensation of light that continues to grow and swell through the ages and into today. We are invited to participate in this movement: to save and to be saved.

Scriptural Reference

Luke 23:26–49

Suggested Additional Sources for Reading

- Victor Shepherd, "Atonement," in *Making Sense of Christian Faith* (Gr Welch, 1987).
- Jon Sobrino, *Christ the Liberator* (Orbis, 2001).
- Jurgen Moltmann, *The Crucified God* (SCM Press, 1974).
- Shusaku Endo, *Silence* (Sophia University, 1969).
- N. T. Wright, *Jesus and the Victory of God* (Augsburg Fortress Press, 1997).
- John D. Caputo, *The Weakness of God: A Theology of the Event* (Indiana Univ. Press, 2006).
- Peter Rollins, *How (Not) to Speak of God—Marks of the Emerging Church* (Paraclete Press, 2006).
- Brian D. McLaren and Tony Campolo, *Adventures in Missing the Point* (Zondervan, 2006).

Suggested Questions for Further Discussion/Thought

1. If you had to choose to live your relationships according to either a system of justice, where every sin must be counted and punished, or a system of love, where we forgive each other from because we love each other, which would you choose? Do you imagine God would do it differently?
2. Is it possible to have love without justice?
3. What is your view of sin? What does sin mean, and how does it affect us?
4. Does sin affect God?
5. Is it possible for God to suffer? How does the idea of a suffering God make you feel? Relieved, scared, or uncertain?
6. Did Jesus have the power to stop his own crucifixion if he wanted to? What does that say about God?
7. Do you see God as an angry judge, a loving parent, or something else? How does that affect your view of Jesus' crucifixion?

Question

6. What happened during the "missing years" of Jesus' life, unaccounted for in the Bible?

Becky Garrison

Who is...
Becky Garrison

I am an urban fly fisher and kayaker.

A. Beats me. While biblical archeologists and historians have pieced together evidence illuminating the life and times of first century Judeans, we have no clue about what Jesus actually did until he begins his ministry.

We can assume that as a good Jewish boy, he probably assisted his father in the carpentry biz though there's no concrete evidence that Jesus became a carpenter. Also, Jesus deviated from the vast majority of his neighbors by receiving some type of an education as evidenced by his vast knowledge of the Hebrew Scriptures.

As Scott Korb points out, "Presumably if you're sitting with scholars discussing theology, you probably know how to read and write."[3] But given that Jesus grew up in an oral culture that valued the spoken over the written word, he might have learned aurally instead.

L. Shannon Moore

A. The only things we know from the Bible about Jesus as a child are found in the book of Luke. As a baby he was named, circumcised, and presented in the temple. Then, at the age of twelve, he accompanied his parents to Jerusalem for the Passover festival and ditched them to chat with the teachers in the Temple.

Now there are some other written gospels that weren't chosen by the early church leaders to make the final cut of the Bible. One of my favorites is called the infancy gospel of Thomas. Written about 125 C.E., it was "devoted to filling the gap left by some of the other gospels."[4] These stories are crazy! For example,

---

3. Scott Korb, *Life in Year One: What the World Was Like in First-Century Palestine* (New York: Riverhead Books, 2010), 17.

4. David R. Cartlidge and David L. Dungan, eds., "The Infancy Gospel of Thomas," in *Documents for the Study of the Gospels* (Minneapolis: Fortress Press, 1994), 86–90.

- Boy Jesus gets in trouble for making clay birds on the Sabbath so he claps his hands, and they turn into real birds and fly away.
- Another kid bumps into Jesus, making him angry. So Jesus yells at him and the kid falls down dead.
- Jesus' father, a carpenter, is making a bed for a rich man and cuts a piece of wood too short. Jesus simply stretches the shorter piece out to match the longer piece.

While these stories make for fun reading, I don't buy them for a second. I think Jesus grew up like all the other boys in his town—going to the synagogue, doing his chores, and so on—and did not possess (or was unaware) of any divine power until after his baptism.

Mark Van Steenwyk

Jesus' life is a big question mark. The gospels mostly tell us about the three years leading up to Jesus' crucifixion. We also know a fair bit about his birth and infancy. We even get an interesting story about Jesus wowing scholars at the temple when he was twelve. But what did he do between the age of twelve and the age of thirty? This is one of those really juicy mysteries that provoke all sorts of speculation.

Most scholars assume that Jesus grew up in Nazareth and learned carpentry. Some say Jesus traveled to India, Nepal, Tibet, or China and soaked up the mojo of Eastern Buddhist mystics. Others say he traveled back to Egypt and learned the wisdom of Egyptian spiritual teachers. But all we really know from the gospels comes from Luke 2:52 where we read, "And Jesus increased in wisdom and in years, and in divine and human favor."

The idea that Jesus had to travel to the East to learn how to be a sage is a bit snobby. Why is it so hard for folks to believe that some peasant kid from occupied Israel could grow up to be the most revered spiritual leader in history without getting some sort of outside help?

The guy was born in a barn! It is only fitting to assume that Jesus grew up humbly and became a blue-collar worker. Throughout his whole life and ministry, the amazing thing about Jesus was that—through it all—he was, from a human perspective, something of a loser. And perhaps even more amazing, he tells us that the kingdom of God belongs to other losers. In other words, we don't need to learn from sages or mystics to be a part of the "big things" that God wants to do in the world today.

Scriptural References

Luke 2:39–52; 3:23

Suggested Additional Sources for Reading

- Elaine Pagels, *Beyond Belief: The Secret Gospel of Thomas* (Vintage, 2004).
- Christopher Moore, *Lamb: The Gospel According to Biff, Christ's Childhood Pal* (Harper, 2003).
- Scott Korb, *Life in Year One: What the World Was Like in First-Century Palestine* (Riverhead, 2010).
- David R. Cartlidge and David L. Dungan, eds., "The Infancy Gospel of Thomas," in *Documents for the Study of the Gospels* (Augsburg Fortress Press, 1994).

Suggested Questions for Further Discussion/Thought

1. Why do you think some people suggest that Jesus' teachings were borrowed from Buddha?
2. Where do you think Jesus went for the eighteen "missing years"?
3. Do you think Jesus possessed, or was aware of, his divine power when he was a child? If so, would it have been in his nature to use them in the ways presented in the infancy gospel of Thomas?

7. How would we actually know if Jesus came again? Wouldn't we just kill him all over again?

Chris Haw

Who is...
Chris Haw

I have a ridiculously affectionate relationship with my dog, Victor.

One's thoughts on Jesus' second coming certainly depend on how one interprets Jesus' continued and future presence. We have biblical references to his being seated at the right hand of the Father (Matthew 22:44), but we also have references to his persistent presence through the poor and "least of these" (Matthew 25:40). Perhaps both, for the modern mind, beg to be interpreted analogically. I am personally and biblically drawn into a cloud of mystery on the matter, both on his presence now and a future eschatological presence. This is among the few clouds I can enter *only* through ritual, liturgy, and tears—not my rationality. My mind has knocked many times, and I have not as of yet been let in.

For René Girard, who thinks that the Christ-story disarms us of our propensity to scapegoat and lynch each other, there is perhaps *some* slightly less likelihood we would kill the lamb of God today—that is, to the extent that the story has disarmed us and permeated our mobs. In places suffering from colonization or the effects of imperialism, it seems there is a heightened inclination toward mob violence (e.g., post-French Rwanda, post-Britain Sudan and Nigeria, post-US Iraq and Afghanistan, etc.). For those of us who are colonizers, invaders, or war makers (or funding them through tax paying), we should know that, if nothing else, our sins are a stumbling block to others, enticing others to rivalry.

Becky Garrison

First-century Judeans had been praying for a mighty Messiah to descend from the heavens and liberate them from the Romans, zealot style. Instead they got a dude from the backwaters of Nazareth. *In lieu* of coming into Jerusalem via a royal procession, he strode in on a donkey, a move that mocked all the pageantry espoused by those in religious and political power. Even those who were drawn to Jesus of Nazareth's message of radical love and forgiveness ran for the hills. However, a few women stood vigil at the foot of the cross. Later they assisted in the burial of the only man who truly embraced them as equals in the kingdom of God.

Ever since Constantine converted to Christianity in 326 C.E., Christians have repeatedly bagged the Beatitudes in their quest to impose an empire-based form of the faith. In the process, those who joined the woman at the foot of the cross by following the way of Jesus often ended up losing their lives. So my strong hunch is that if Jesus of Nazareth would appear today, he wouldn't look anything like what we "think" a messiah should be and people would reject him yet again.

Peter J. Walker

A. There's an awful movie from the early '90s called *The Judas Project* about this scenario. I'm having flashbacks.

I can't imagine many "patriotic Americans" feeling *enthused* about Jesus reiterating exhortations to give everything to the poor, turn the other cheek, and love our enemies. After all, we've created a subculture dominated by self-defense theology (we call it "apologetics") and cultural separation from the world (we call it "holy living") that undermines everything about Jesus' worldly ministry, including his willingness to die on the cross. Would we kill Jesus? Maybe, if he tried to pass gun control legislation. More likely, we'd marginalize him into silence: We'd pick and choose Bible verses to undermine him, preach sermons decrying his disrespect for church tradition and family values, and go on talk radio to mock and belittle his lack of practicality, piety, and patriotism.

And Jesus may have actually believed he was returning much sooner than we've come to assume: "There are some standing here who will not taste death before they see the Son of Man coming in his kingdom" (Matthew 16:28). That didn't happen.

Edgar Whisenant published *88 Reasons Why the Rapture Will Be in 1988*. When Jesus didn't show, he followed with *Why Christ Must Return in 1989*. Doesn't "*must*" sound like an order? Maybe instead of spending so much time worrying about Christ's return, we should focus on cleaning up our mess. War, poverty, genocide, extremism, disease, and ecological abuse all undermine Christian testimony as the "light of the world," because the church has too often communicated indifference. In Matthew 7:19–20, Jesus said, "Every tree that does not bear good fruit is cut down and thrown into the fire. Thus you will know them by their fruits." We may have a long wait, and we need to grow a lot more fruit.

Tripp Fuller

The second coming of Jesus is an interesting phrase because it is very confusing when it is taken out of its original context. The early Christians who used it were trying to develop a way of explaining how Jesus could have been resurrected without God's kingdom fully arrived. Pretty weird sounding these days, but for them they imagined history being two completely different ages: old creation, in which sin and death were present throughout, and new creation, in which sin and death are defeated and the world would be under the perfectly just and peaceful reign of God.

The transition between the two ages was the resurrection of all the dead. When Jesus was raised alone and the kingdom of God had not fully come, they came to understand Jesus as the first fruits of the larger harvest to come and the kingdom of God as present but still coming. When we consider the question in this context, we can say that when Jesus comes again it won't be as before, an exceptional member of the old creation but as the resurrected host of new creation.

We won't kill him again because his "second coming" is a symbol for the arrival of the new creation and the end of the old, a time when sin has been conquered and death has been defeated. What the question, and the early church's reasoning, point out is that the world we live in is not the world we believe God wants. Our hope and our challenge as Christians are to live toward new creation. We can't make everything right in our world, or even ourselves! But we can celebrate and anticipate what God has done for us in Christ and participate in the new creation's coming by living in the way of Jesus.

R. M. Keelan Downton

Who is...
R. M. Keelan Downton

Going by our middle names is something of a family tradition.

I've sometimes thought that the fascination many Christians experience at some point in their journey with "the end times" is a rather strange way to affirm belief in the resurrection. Jesus "coming again" in this sense is hardly worth the wait if you could miss it while trying to finish one more Sudoku on your cell phone.

The point of stories about irresponsible wedding attendants or attention-deficit farmers is not to get us to speak a particular set of phrases to every people group but rather to provoke us to participation in God's intentions for the world today rather than putting it off until some point in the future. From that perspective, Jesus is not *coming*, but is *here*.

This is true not simply in Jesus' promise to be "in the midst of" two or three followers but in the more immediate presence of persons in need. But what if Jesus were to incarnate again on the sly? Well, he was an Afro-Asiatic Jew tortured to death as a terrorist for inciting revolt against an ancient world superpower, so chances are he'd have a tough time getting on an airplane.

Scriptural References

Matthew 5:14; 16:27–28; 17:19–20; 27:55–61; Mark 15:40–48; Luke 21:31–33; 23:49–56; 1 Corinthians 15:20ff

Suggested Additional Sources for Reading

- Rene Girard and James G. Williams, eds., *The Girard Reader* (Crossroad, 1996).
- Stephen Prothero, *American Jesus* (Farrar, Straus and Giroux, 2004).
- Oren Jacoby, director, *Constantine's Sword* (Storyville Films, 2007). DVD available at http://www.constantinessword.com.
- Richard W. Fox, *Jesus in America* (HarperOne, 2005).
- Leonard Sweet and Frank Viola, *The Jesus Manifesto* (available at http://www.thejesusmanifesto.com).
- Brian D. McLaren and Tony Campolo, *Adventures in Missing the Point* (Zondervan, 2006).
- Marcus Borg and N. T. Wright, *The Meaning of Jesus: Two Visions* (HarperOne, 2007).
- Glenn Shuck, *Marks of the Beast: The Left Behind Novels and the Struggle for Evangelical Identity* (NYU Press, 2004).
- James H. Barden, director, *The Judas Project* (Judas Project, 1990).

Suggested Questions for Further Discussion/Thought

1. Could Jesus have been wrong about his imminent return, or are we misinterpreting?
2. Does the idea of Jesus' return make me feel hopeful or terrified?
3. If Jesus is returning soon, how does that change the way we view God? Our faith?
4. How should we prepare for Christ's return? Is that preparation different if the return is *literal* versus *figurative*? How is it different?
5. What do you think Jesus would look like if he came back today?

8. Why should I believe that Jesus was resurrected? What does it mean to the Christian faith if he wasn't resurrected?

Peter J. Walker

The church has consistently affirmed the literal resurrection throughout history, defending it as central dogma. I affirm it too, but I have a hunch that you can personally know Jesus, either way. Theologian Rudolf Bultmann argued that the literal resurrection was less important than the story behind the myth. He believed that the power of the resurrection for modern believers is in its theological meaning—in what it said about the nature of God and the human condition. Bultmann stressed the importance of *choosing* faith rather than believing faith is somehow inevitable once "proven" legitimate.

So you don't *have* to believe that Jesus of Nazareth was resurrected. But if you can't at least believe that Jesus *might* have been resurrected, maybe we should talk about why. To me, a worldview bound by some notion of rigid Newtonian physics seems less creative, less dynamic, and less interesting than faith open to the supernatural. It's another kind of fundamentalism. I want to be able to dream dreams and hear whispers in the dark, even if I never see someone walk on water or heal the blind.

Deism, keeping God passive and separate from the workings of creation, certainly makes the problem of suffering more palatable. But there's something about Jesus more compelling than a moral philosophy or historic "high point" of humanity. There's more to Jesus than wisdom. I choose belief in a God who "can"—a God willing to be weak, to suffer and die. It's very existential. If God did or did not, that is less important to me. A God who at least *can* is a God who can reach me.

Amy Reeder Worley

Most of us have heard the atheist critique of the resurrection of Jesus. "Zombie Jesus" is one pop culture reference to the secular humanist/atheist's view of what they claim is the utter ridiculousness of the Christian belief that Jesus of Nazareth was crucified, died, and came back to life on the third day. Likewise, my disbelief in a literal resurrection of Jesus was one of many reasons I left the faith for years. I cannot adhere to a "magic" religion that requires belief in scientifically impossible events. So Zombie Jesus wasn't for me.

When I came back to the study of Christianity as an adult, after a foray into Buddhism and Yoga, I came to a new understanding of the resurrection. Well, actually I came back to an old understanding of the Christian resurrection, one that predates the post-Enlightenment religious literalism. Like the many religious resurrection stories before Christianity (e.g., Isis and Osiris), Jesus' resurrection is a metaphor for the very real process of dying to one's old life and living again in Jesus.

Sometimes referred to as "participatory atonement," many nonevangelical Christians take the Pauline approach that we metaphorically die to our old, unenlightened ways and then rise again filled with the spirit of Christ. In Galatians 2:19–20 Paul writes, "I have been crucified with Christ; and it is no longer I who live, but it is Christ who lives in me."

In this way, the resurrection of Christ is central to the Christian faith. Practicing Christians try to model Jesus by dying to our selfish, distracted ways and remaking ourselves in Christ's image. So although the resurrection is of utmost importance to Christians, we need not take it literally in order to believe.

Jarrod McKenna

Who is...
Jarrod McKenna

I hate Scrabble (I'm dyslexic).

Last time I was arrested for resisting the ongoing wars in Iraq and Afghanistan the police officer said to me, and I quote, "You need to realize that war is money. And money makes the world go round. The sooner you realize that, the sooner you can fit in like the rest of us."

If Jesus wasn't resurrected, the police officer is right. The powers that crucified our Lord are right. We are still stuck in sin and in a closed sinful system that is fueled by, and profits from, the blood of our oppressed sisters and brothers. Our Lord's nonviolent way of the cross is not vindicated victorious over evil. There is no new world of God's kingdom breaking in, of which our Lord Jesus is the first fruits. Our faith is futile and we are to be pitied.

The hope of oppressed Jews of Jesus' day was *not* to be liberated from God's good creation; rather, they hoped for a material liberation from all injustice, violence, and oppression (Isaiah 2:2–4, 9:1–7, 11:6–9, 35:5–6, 60:17–19, and Micah 4:1–3, among others). They longed for that day when "God's Great Cosmic Clean-Up"[5] would kick-start with the righteous being raised to inherit the world-put-right. With a rationale echoing the words of the police officer, the Sadducees and Herodians sold out the revolutionary hope of resurrection

---

5. John Dominic Crossan's expression for the Kingdom of God.

because bodily resurrection will always threaten those who practice "spiritu-alities" that collaborate and profit from the powers' oppression.

The scandal of the bodily resurrection of Jesus (which N. T. Wright has persuasively argued as the most conceivable explanation for the birth and shape of the early church) is that the Jewish revolutionary hope has started! Yet scandalously, it's started through a crucified, nonviolent messiah in the middle of history. Now all creation waits in eager expectation for us to walk in the resurrection by taking up our cross, in the power of the Spirit, and wit-ness to the end of all injustice, violence, oppression, and evil, which has now started because Jesus is risen from the grave.

L. Shannon Moore

Who is...
L. Shannon Moore

My most hated words (in order) are moist, loaf, and wipe.

We can look at the resurrection metaphorically. When we have Christ in our lives, the "old" self is resurrected into the "new" self. The worm becomes a butterfly; the egg becomes a bird; and the lost becomes the found. I get it.

But what about the physical resurrection of Jesus? My childhood Sun-day school teacher would faint if she were to hear me say this, but I don't think it matters if Jesus rose from the dead or not. I do believe that Jesus, in human form, was the Son of God. And if he did rise from the grave, defeat-ing death and sin and all things evil, I have no trouble believing that either. But if archaeologists were to discover his body in a tomb outside of Jerusalem tomorrow, it would not affect my faith. At all. Even though Christianity was born on that very idea (and acknowledging that untold millions have died defending that belief), I don't strive to pattern my life on the resurrection. I work toward following what Jesus taught, what he *said* and how he *lived* rather than on what happened after he died.

To be clear—until archaeologists actually do produce concrete, undeni-able proof to the contrary, I choose to believe in the resurrection as it is told to us in the scriptures. But do I think that one has to believe in the resurrection to be a Christ follower? No.

Mark Van Steenwyk

The Apostle Paul wrote, "If Christ has not been raised, your faith is futile and you are still in your sins" (1 Corinthians 15:17). He also said that if Jesus wasn't raised, we won't be either. This would, he suggests, make our faith useless.

For the most part, I agree with Paul. The resurrection of Jesus not only gives us hope that we too will ultimately cheat death, but it also gives us hope that everything will be renewed—all death, degradation, sin, brokenness, sickness, and injustice will be transformed into something amazing.

Without that, would our faith be, as Paul suggests, useless? I'm not so sure. I'd still follow Jesus even if I were an atheist. Jesus has a lot to say about how to live in the here and now. Without the resurrection, we'd be left with a deeply challenging way to live our lives; a way that calls us to love our enemies, pursue justice, and seek peace. But we'd labor not knowing if we will be vindicated in our struggle. We'd go through life feeling the weight of our sins and the injustices of the world. That would be hard, but we could do far worse.

It would be worse for us to gain hope in the resurrection of Jesus and use it as an excuse for inaction. Because Jesus has defeated death, he is the true Lord of the whole world. Therefore we, his followers, have a job to do; we must act as his heralds, announcing his lordship to the entire world. Jesus is raised, therefore God's new world has begun, and therefore we are invited to be not only beneficiaries of that new world but participants in making it happen.

In his book *Worship and Politics*, Rafael Avila writes, "The resurrection is the ultimate basis for rebellion."[6] Ultimately, the resurrection gives us hope that, if we challenge the brokenness in the world, we will win.

Scriptural References

Isaiah 2:2–4; 9:1–7; 11:6–9; 35:5–6; 60:17–19; Micah 4:1–3; Matthew 28:1–10; Mark 16:1–11; Luke 24:1–12; John 20:1–8; Romans 6:3–4; 8; 12:2; 1 Corinthians 15; Galatians 2:19–20

Suggested Additional Sources for Reading

- Karen Armstrong, *The Case for God* (Knopf, 2009).
- John Shelby Spong, *Rescuing the Bible from Fundamentalism: A Bishop Rethinks the Meaning of Scripture* (HarperSanFrancisco, 1991).
- Marcus Borg and John Dominic Crossan, *The First Paul: Reclaiming the Radical Visionary Behind the Church's Conservative Icon* (HarperOne, 2009).

---

6. Rafael Ávila, *Worship and Politics* (Maryknoll, NY: Orbis Books, 1981).

- N. T. Wright, *Jesus and the Victory of God* (Augsburg Fortress Press, 1997).
- Rudolph Bultmann, *Jesus Christ and Mythology* (Scribner, 1958).
- Marcus J. Borg, *The Heart of Christianity: Rediscovering a Life of Faith* (HarperSanFrancisco, 2003).
- Marcus J. Borg, *Meeting Jesus Again for the First Time: The Historical Jesus and the Heart of Contemporary Faith* (HarperSanFrancisco, 1994).
- Vintage Faith Church: http://www.vintagechurch.org.
- N. T. Wright, *The Resurrection of the Son of God* (SPCK, 2003).
- Lee C. Camp, *Mere Discipleship* (Brazos Press, 2003).
- Marcus Borg and N. T. Wright, *The Meaning of Jesus* (HarperOne, 2007).
- Robert B. Stewart, ed., *The Resurrection of Jesus: John Dominic Crossan and N. T. Wright in Dialogue* (Fortress Press, 2005).
- N. T. Wright, *Surprised by Hope* (HarperOne, 2008).
- Simon Barrow, *Threatened with Resurrection* (Darton, Longman, & Todd, 2008).

Suggested Questions for Further Discussion/Thought

1. Have you ever considered that being a Christian does not require belief in the literal resurrection of Jesus? Do you think that Christians must believe in the literal resurrection?
2. How does taking a metaphorical view of the resurrection affect your faith?
3. What were you originally taught about the resurrection?
4. How can we "know" Jesus—*God*, for that matter—without letting the beliefs, opinions or experiences of others overinfluence us?
5. Do we have to be sure of what we believe? What does it look like *not* to decide?
6. Is there a difference between being a "Christian" and being a "Christ follower?"
7. How revolutionary is your understanding of the resurrection?

Question

9. A woman in Mark 7:25-30 and Matthew 15:21-28 asks Jesus to heal her daughter, but his first response is to deny her help and call her a dog. Isn't this a cruel, and pretty un-Christlike, response?

David Lose

Who is...
David Lose

I'm a sixth-generation Lutheran pastor.

A. There are two options most readers flee to when trying to make sense of Jesus' interaction with this Gentile woman. Either Jesus didn't really mean it (supposedly, the Greek word translated as "dog" was a term of endearment, as in "little dog" or "puppy") or he was testing her faith. Both options are, I think, bogus. "Puppy" wouldn't have been any less insulting than "dog," and nowhere else does Jesus test faith in such a heartless way.

But most Christians opt for one of these interpretations anyway because they can't imagine a third option: that Jesus was being a jerk. But are you being a jerk if you're just acting like everyone else? Odds are, Jesus' attitude toward this foreign woman was common among Jewish men, even considered proper, as evidenced by the disciples.

Funny thing, though: If Jesus' mission is only for the house of Israel, why is he travelling so far abroad? Tyre and Sidon are way north of Judea and Galilee, Jesus' usual haunts. So I wonder—could it be that Jesus' mission has gone and ventured ahead of his inherited attitudes? Might it be that the Spirit that drove him into the wilderness is now driving him across barriers, social and ethnic as well as geographical? If so, then perhaps Jesus learns something this day.

Perhaps this Gentile woman teaches Jesus a lesson and actually extends his vision of just how radically inclusive his mission is. If so, then let us give thanks for fierce mothers and pushy women, for we who are also Gentiles have much for which to be thankful.

L. Shannon Moore

Jesus' response was to this woman was un-*Jesus*-like, particularly in the way modern-day people tend to think of Jesus—doe eyed, gentle, meek, and mild. But his response was not un-*Christ*like as far as he was concerned, because Jesus initially saw himself as a Christ or Messiah for the Jewish people—not the Gentiles.

Before his encounter with the Gentile woman in question, Jesus does heal a Gentile man who is possessed with demons. However, when the man begs Jesus to allow him to become one of his followers, Jesus denies his request and sends him home.

For a more direct example, look at Matthew 10:5–6, where Jesus sends his disciples out on a mission trip. He says to them, "Go nowhere among the Gentiles . . . but go rather to the lost sheep of the house of Israel." Tough luck, *goys*.

Back then, both women and Gentiles were considered "less than" Jewish men. So naturally, when a Gentile woman approaches Jesus to heal her daughter, he is not all that interested in listening to her. But the cool thing about this story is this oppressed woman's persistence. She just keeps shouting after him, refusing to be ignored. And when he compares her to a dog, she refuses to be dismissed, reminding him that even dogs are fed by their masters. So he healed her daughter.

I think this exchange was an eye-opener for Jesus. He was able to see that he still had things to learn about his call. He, who ate with sinners and outcasts, saw that the doors to God's kingdom were open wider than even he had realized.

R. M. Keelan Downton

There's an Irish phrase, "winding you up," which describes someone exaggerating (or just making up) a story in order to evoke a strong emotive response from someone else. It's a kind of conversational game that can be immensely entertaining for those who catch on to what is happening and join in on the "winding" until the target realizes he's been had.

Though this could be done in a mean-spirited way, it's practiced most often among friends—I think because it communicates a subtle kind of intimacy: I know what makes you angry, what things you're gullible about, and what things you get so caught up in you won't realize what I'm doing. I've often wondered if Jesus is up to something like that when he renames the most unpredictable disciple, Peter, "rock."

When this woman persists in seeking help from Jesus he is not cracking jokes, but he is doing something similar that makes a point by walking around the edge rather than addressing it directly. The story is present to contradict anyone who wished to restrict the gospel proclamation to Israel as much as the story of Thomas wanting to touch Jesus' wounds after the resurrection is present to contradict anyone who would say the resurrection encounters were visions or illusions.

By drawing attention to the prevailing ideas about Canaanites, Jesus sets up a call and response where the apparent outsider demonstrates she is more of an insider than many of those who are apparently within the house of Israel. This encounter also suggests the possibility that Jesus did not wake up with a predetermined agenda in his head each day. Jesus could be surprised by people and engage in real relationships where love gets worked out in the midst of the unexpected.

Chris Haw

A. To understand this text we must see that it includes a non-Jewish woman. In relation to the question as to "whether Jesus changed his mind," some interpreters have argued that, in this story, the faith and witness of a woman changed Jesus' Israel-centric mission.

That seems just as likely and fruitful as my interpretation—which is that his statement is a literary device meant to repeat in the culturally sensitive (perhaps Jewish) reader's mind what they were likely already objecting: It is abnormal for a good Jewish prophet to heal anyone outside of Israel, especially a woman. As we know from Jesus' proclamation at the synagogue that Ezekiel went to Gentiles to heal, healing people from a different nationality was a touchy subject to Jews—and enflamed them to attempt killing him. So as a literary device, the author puts in the mouth of Christ a reminder of how offensive his act was—how much he is going against the social script of the day—and then he does it.

Peter J. Walker

Who is...
Peter J. Walker

I played a bit role in Lifetime Television's Fifteen and Pregnant, *starring Kirsten Dunst.*

A. Yes, it seems pretty un-Christlike, especially if we try to keep Jesus caged by our own modern worldviews. Many conservatives want a "hawk" who turns over tables and wages holy war, while liberals want an eco-friendly "dove" who will leave that poor fig tree in Mark 11 alone! Undeniably, there is a controversial character to Jesus' mission that frustrates our attempts to reconcile him as lion or lamb, soldier or hippie. In Luke 12:51 Jesus says, "Do you think I came to bring peace to the earth? No, I tell you, but rather division!" Matthew 10:35 echoes this: "For I have come to set a man against his father, and a daughter against her mother."

But what if we don't even *try* to justify Jesus' actions by shaping him to fit our agendas? What if Jesus was tired and short on patience the day he withdrew to Tyre? Is it impious to suggest that Jesus Christ may not have always got it right on the first try? Maybe this was a teaching moment for him, echoing Jesus' own astonishment at the centurion in Matthew 8 whose faith exceeded his expectations. The Canaanite woman's response in Matthew 15 grabbed Jesus' attention and reversed his response: "Woman, great is your faith!"

I don't think it's necessary or even ethical to defend words that seem so blatantly unkind. I have witnessed too many pastors indirectly endorse bad behavior for the sake of getting Jesus off the hook here. Jesus probably doesn't need our protection. The Canaanite woman probably does.

Jarrod McKenna

A. If we don't understand what our Lord has chosen us to be a part of—the fulfillment and transformation of the Hebraic hopes—this story will just read like Jesus is a racist and calls this woman a bitch.

Our Lord has just fed five thousand in Matthew's gospel despite his attempts to lose the crowds and grieve the loss of John the Baptist. With the retelling dripping with resonance to the Exodus story, Jesus provides bread like manna from heaven with twelve baskets left over, like the twelve tribes of Israel. Is Jesus really telling the woman he doesn't have enough "bread" for her considering the leftovers in Matthew 14:20? What is this darkness that our pillar of fire Jesus leads us through?

"Destroy them totally . . . show them no mercy," "do not look on them with compassion," "you will wipe their names from under heaven." These disturbing phrases come from the rally cry describing how the twelve tribes liberated from under pharaoh's oppression are to deal with the seven stronger nations whose land they will take. In short, genocide is not a weapon ruled out in the guerrilla warfare of Deuteronomy 7. And those seven tribes of Canna (Acts 13:19) that they are told to wipe out are represented by this woman, who Matthew, in a strange move, calls "a Canaanite."

Why strange? Sylvia Keesmaat (who everyone should read) notes calling this woman a "Canaanite" in Jesus' day would be like you calling your

Swedish friend a "Viking," your French friend a "Gaul," or your Irish friend a "Celt." Matthew wants us to see—to the shock of the disciples—their understanding of the Exodus, outsiders, and God is being transformed by Jesus as he dramatically brings them into Deuteronomy 7 being renegotiated in conversation with this woman.

To quote Keesmaat, "the hatred of the Gentiles has become the healing of the Gentiles." Matthew's gospel punctuates this point by having this interaction be immediately followed by Jesus feeding the masses. But this time the leftovers are not twelve baskets, representing Israel, but seven baskets, representing the tribes of Canna (Matthew 15:34–37).

In Jesus, genocidal liberation from enemies is transformed into generous liberation that *includes* enemies. Only Jesus shows us what it is to be Christlike, to love in a transformative way like God does (Matthew 5:43–48; Romans 5:8).

Scriptural References

Deuteronomy 7; Matthew 5:43–48; 8:5–10; 8:38–9:1; 10:5–6; 10:35; 14:13–21; 15:21–39; Mark 5:1–20; 11:12–21; Luke 8:26–39; 12:49; Romans 5:8

Suggested Additional Sources for Reading

- Elisabeth Schüssler Fiorenza, *In Memory of Her* (Crossroad, 1983).
- André Trocmé, *Jesus and the Nonviolent Revolution* (Herald Press, 1973).
- Everything written by Sylvia Keesmaat and her husband, Brian Walsh

Suggested Questions for Further Discussion/Thought

1. Shannon makes a distinction between *Jesus* and *Christ*. What's the difference?
2. Do you think Jesus changed his attitude about Gentiles after his encounter with this woman, or was this a one-time exception?
3. Can we imagine that Jesus—who we confess was both human and divine—learned something? What does imagining that gain us? What does it risk?
4. What does it mean to call Jesus "perfect"? Does "perfection" equal "truth"?
5. How does it impact my own life and self-concept if I see Jesus as someone who grew, matured, and developed rather than simply arrived all at once?

10. Does it really matter if Jesus was born to a virgin or not? What if Mary wasn't a virgin or if Joseph (or someone else) was the father?

Amy Reeder Worley

Although many Christians disagree with me, I don't think belief in the literal virgin birth of Jesus is necessary to Christianity. Jesus was both fully human and fully divine whether or not he was born of a virgin. Jesus taught that we may all enter the kingdom of God, even though we're conceived by the usual means. Moreover, in describing his own relationship to God, Jesus did not rely on the virgin birth as proof of his divinity.

It is impossible to ever really know whether Mary was a virgin when she became pregnant with Jesus. However, we do know generally that conception requires that a sperm connect with an ovum to create an embryo. Could God create a virgin birth? Probably. Did God impregnate Mary by the Holy Spirit? Let's just say this—it wasn't necessary for God to do so for Jesus' message to be true.

As a woman and a feminist, my view of the virgin birth is complicated. Throughout the history of the church, the virgin birth has resulted in a view among some that women who are not sexually active should be adulated while sexually active women should be subjugated. This is often referred to in feminist scholarship as the "Madonna or the Whore" dichotomy. This dichotomy has caused sexually active women to feel unworthy of God's love and unable to fully experience it. The virgin birth also emphasizes the Divine's masculine attributes—the ability to cause pregnancy while ignoring the femininity of the Divine. These views have wounded the church universal, in particular its female members.

Jesus, however, included women in his ministry without reference to their sexual status. He bestowed mercy upon an adulterous woman. It was some combination of women to whom Jesus' resurrection was revealed. Accordingly, while we are certainly free to believe in a literal virgin birth, to do so is unnecessary.

Sherri Emmons

Who is...
Sherri Emmons

I've been to Jordan, China, Australia, Jamaica, and Mexico. I really want to go to Bhutan.

A. It doesn't matter to me if Jesus was born to a virgin. There are so many ancient tales in the Middle East of gods fathering children with virgins—the Greeks, Romans, and Egyptians all had such tales. So perhaps Jesus' original followers felt the need to "up" their prophet with that credential as well.

What does matter is what Jesus taught—love your enemies, love God with all your heart and soul, take care of those in need, and use your talents to serve God. The Christ I follow is one who calls me to act justly, speak truthfully, work tirelessly, and love endlessly. He lived those truths, even when it was hard and dangerous, and ultimately he died for them. That's what is important.

Peter J. Walker

A. It's easy to take for granted the early church's universal acknowledgement of Jesus' virgin conception based on its centrality in church tradition. But supported by scripture alone, it's surprising that Matthew and Luke were so unquestionably convinced, given that there is no other reference in the entire New Testament. The gospel accounts of Mark and John seem uninterested, and Paul didn't find it critical to his own apologetics.

"He [Jesus] was the son (as was thought) of Joseph" (Luke 3:23). *So it was thought* was good enough for Luke, but what about modern readers? Why are the genealogies so vastly different while both build through Joseph as Jesus' father? Was Joseph able to "adopt" Jesus into the Davidic line? Was Mary's virginity *constructed* to emphasize Jesus' divinity?

It surprises my friends when I ask these questions but still deliberately affirm the virgin conception. I am simultaneously aware of its unresolved difficulties and mindful of the power in its imagery and liturgical history. Many church doctrines have been diligently protected for two thousand years, and while I personally find little to call "nonnegotiable," I readily admit my own limitations.

Far more gifted, brilliant theologians have done battle before me, and in most cases, it doesn't hurt me to hold onto orthodox theology (lightly, with

43

unclenched hands). I try to avoid rejecting traditional dogma outright unless it is used to exclude, abuse, or oppress others. In this vein, Mary's virginity has certainly had a complicated historical impact on women: simultaneously affirming their importance while narrowly restricting female sexual identity.

Scriptural References

Matthew 1; Luke 1:26–38; 3

Suggested Additional Sources for Reading

- Elizabeth A. Johnson, *She Who Is* (Crossroad, 1992).
- Sue Monk-Kidd, *The Dance of the Dissident Daughter* (HarperSanFrancisco, 1996).
- Raymond Brown, *The Birth of the Messiah: A Commentary of the Infancy Narratives in the Gospels of Matthew and Luke* (Yale Univ. Press, 1999).
- Yigal Levin, "Jesus, 'Son of God' and 'Son of David': The 'Adoption' of Jesus into the Davidic Line," *Journal for the Study of the New Testament* 28, no. 4 (June 2006).
- Marcus J. Borg and John Dominic Crossan, *The First Christmas: What the Gospels Really Teach about Jesus's Birth* (HarperOne, 2009).
- Marguerite Rigoglioso, *The Cult of Divine Birth in Ancient Greece* (Palgrave Macmillan, 2009).
- J. Gresham Machen, *The Virgin Birth of Christ* (Harper and Bros., 1930).
- Roger Underwood, "The Virgin Birth: Why I Believe," *DisciplesWorld*, December 2003, 3–4.
- Jimmy R. Watson, "The Virgin Birth: Does It Matter?," *DisciplesWorld*, December 2003, 3, 5.

Suggested Questions for Further Discussion/Thought

1. Do you think the virgin birth story has affected the way the church views women?
2. If the virgin birth story is not literally true, how does that change your view of Jesus?
3. If you believe in the virgin birth, what impact does it have on your faith?
4. There are all sorts of questions in scripture that leave us hanging. How might answering those questions impact your spiritual journey? Which questions of faith are nonnegotiable for you?
5. What if Jesus was actually Joseph's biological son? Could Jesus still be God?

11. Did Jesus really live a life without any sin? What do we base this on? And does it matter? Why?

Pablo A. Jiménez

A. For people who understand sin as transgression, the idea of Jesus' "sinlessness" is ludicrous. Could anyone, including Jesus, live without sticking his or her hand in the forbidden cookie jar? Of course not! And once this basic tenet of the Christian faith falls to the ground, all other theological constructions must also tumble down.

Understanding sin as transgression leaves us with only two options. The first one is a Christology of moral example, where Jesus of Nazareth is viewed as an exemplary person, similar to Gandhi or Mother Theresa. The second option is a Christology that denies Jesus' humanity, affirming that his divine nature empowered him to live without transgressing.

However, the New Testament has another view of sin. It affirms that sin is a force or a state, more than a violation of the law. Being "in sin" implies being under the influence of the forces of death. Viewed from this standpoint, Jesus was indeed without sin because he was totally committed with God and with God's project for the world, God's kingdom or realm. His commitment was so strong that the forces of death had no power over him. His faithfulness was such that he ended up dying in a cross. The death of the innocent one unmasked the forces of death, exposing them in public defeat (Colossians 2:15).

This particular understanding of the faith leads me, then, to affirm Jesus' victory over sin.

Phil Snider

Who is...
Phil Snider

Unlike 99.9 percent of the people I know, I can't stand cheese.

A. The idea that Jesus lived a life without sin was a fairly common assumption in the Christian scriptures. There are several verses that highlight this idea, and it's probably seen most clearly in Hebrews 4:15: "For we do not have a high priest [Jesus Christ] who is unable to sympathize with our weaknesses, but we have one who in every respect has been tested as we are, yet without sin."

Believing that Jesus was sinless has been very important for Christians. It implies that Jesus met the requirements necessary to be an unblemished lamb fit for sacrifice. Though I understand the reasons why many Christians interpret Jesus' death as a sacrifice for our sins, I don't think this is a helpful doctrine (mostly because it implies that God can only save us through violence).

To be honest, if I found out that Jesus told some white lies and used some foul language, it wouldn't bother me very much. I'm perfectly fine with the idea that Jesus could've had a girlfriend or been married, even though the historical likelihood of that is very minimal. In the end, what draws me toward Jesus is the vision he proclaimed as well as his courage to stand true to his convictions even in the face of death. This is what has transformed my own life, and it's one of the main reasons I affirm him as the Christ.

José F. Morales Jr.

Who is...
José F. Morales Jr.

I am a techno/house DJ.

"When anyone brings from the herd or flock a fellowship offering to the LORD . . . , it must be *without defect or blemish* to be acceptable." (Leviticus 22:21, NIV)

"For you know that it was not with perishable things such as silver or gold that you were redeemed . . . but with the precious blood of Christ, a lamb *without blemish or defect*." (1 Peter 1:18–19, NIV)

"For we do not have a high priest who is unable to sympathize with our weaknesses, but we have one who has been tempted in every way, just as we are—yet was *without sin*." (Hebrew 4:15, NIV)

The defense for a sinless Jesus is indispensible if you believe that substitutionary atonement is the cornerstone of the gospel. Substitutionary atonement asserts that God's justice needed to be satisfied with a *perfect* sacrifice, so God offered his Son, a "lamb without blemish," for our sins.

I personally have some issues with this view. Nevertheless, I still believe that Jesus was sinless, but not for substitutionary reasons. (Sorry, fellow critical Christians! I guess I can't shake off my early indoctrination.)

My reason for a Christ without sin stems from my definition of "sin." There's a difference between "sin" and "sins." "Sins" (plural) means "missing the mark" or "mistakes." The sixteenth century reformer Martin Luther reminded the church that "sin" (singular) means "separation"—from God, each other, and creation (Genesis 3).

I believe that Jesus, the lamb of God, was without sin because he walked the earth in complete union with God. As John's Jesus declared, "Whoever has seen me has seen the Father" (John 14:9); and "The Father and I are one" (John 10:30).

And this sinless Jesus saves us by overcoming the separation and bringing us back in union with God. Paul declared that God "reconciled us to himself through Christ" (2 Corinthians 5:18). And Jesus prayed for us all, saying, "I ask . . . that they may all be one. As you, Father, are in me and I am in you" (John 17:20–21).

L. Shannon Moore

A. If we take what the Bible has to say at face value, then Jesus did live without sin. The New Testament says explicitly that Jesus was without sin. But here's the deal: What is sin? If we want to get nitpicky about it then Jesus may not have been as perfect as we imagined.

Looking at the laws of Moses, Jesus walks on thin ice. He does not obey the command to be fruitful and multiply. He entices James and John to leave their father's fishing enterprise *and* he ignores his own mother when she wants to speak to him, thus breaking the command to honor our parents. Jesus allows his disciples to pluck grain on the Sabbath. He, arguably, performs magic tricks (we call them miracles, but seriously—turning water into wine doesn't exactly serve humanity's greatest needs).

Even if we step outside of the Jewish laws, Jesus doesn't always act like a perfect person should. He is mean to a woman who asks him to heal her daughter, basically calling her a dog. He even contradicts his own teaching against being angry when he drives those who are conducting business in the Temple out into the streets.

If these examples seem silly, think about how often we judge others similarly. Only God, who knows our hearts and intentions, can determine with certainty what sin is. We only need to know that it is this same God who forgives us as well.

Scriptural References

Genesis 1:28; 3; Exodus 3:14; 20:12; Leviticus 22; Deuteronomy 18:10; Isaiah 53:9; Matthew 4:21–22; 5:21; Mark 3:31; 7:25–30; 10:17–18; Luke 6:1–15; John 2:1–11, 13–16; 10:22–30; 14:5–14; 17:20–26; 2 Corinthians 5:21; Hebrews 4:14–16; 1 Peter 1:13–25; 2:22; 1 John 1:8–10; 3:5

Suggested Additional Sources for Reading

- Marcus Borg, *Jesus: Uncovering the Life, Teachings, and Relevance of a Religious Revolutionary* (HarperSanFrancisco, 2006).
- Mark Dever, "Nothing But the Blood," *Christianity Today*, May 2006. http://www.christianitytoday.com/ct/2006/may/9.29.html.
- Stanley J. Grenz, "Sin: The Destruction of Community," in *Theology for the Community of God* (Eerdmans, 2000).
- William C. Placher, "How Does Jesus Save?," *Christian Century*, June 2, 2009. http://findarticles.com/p/articles/mi_m1058/is_11_126/ai _n32106634.
- Peter K. Stevenson and Stephen I. Wright, *Preaching the Atonement* (T & T Clark, 2005).
- Thomas F. Torrance, *Atonement: The Person and Work of Christ* (IVP Academic, 2009).

Suggested Questions for Further Discussion/Thought

1. What is your definition of sin? Does it have more to do with the behavior of individuals (i.e., telling a lie, rushing to war, etc.) or the condition that human beings find themselves in (i.e., the recognition that human beings are flawed and inevitably make mistakes)?
2. Is God the only one who can "determine with certainty what sin is"?
3. Do you consider the examples of Jesus' behavior that the writer suggested to be sins? Why or why not?
4. Have you ever thought about the dynamics of systemic sin (i.e., the ways that social structures benefit some people and hurt other people)? How might systemic sin diminish God's dreams for all creation?
5. How important is the notion of a sinless Christ for you? Why?
6. What's Jesus' role in salvation? And what does "salvation" mean to you?
7. What is the difference between "magic" and "miracle?"

Question

12. Why did Jesus cry out "My God, my God, why have you forsaken me?" from the cross? Did God really abandon him? If so, doesn't this mean that Jesus wasn't actually God?

David Lose

Who is... David Lose

When I was a kid, my greatest ambition was to be in the Olympics . . . in any sport, and as each Olympics comes and goes, I have to cross off more sports that I'm too old for!

A. Early in its history, the Christian church realized it had four accounts of Jesus that, while similar in many respects, were also quite different in others. In response, some favored choosing one gospel—a guy named Marcion wanted to keep Luke and get rid of the rest. Others wanted to blend them together—a guy named Tatian harmonized them into one seamless volume that was pretty popular for about two hundred years. Eventually, however, the church decided that we actually got a richer, *truer* picture of Jesus by having four distinct perspectives. Think of a complex sculpture and how you will see and appreciate it differently depending on where you're standing.

The diversity and richness of the four gospel witnesses is nowhere more evident than in their distinct portrayals of Jesus' passion. John's Jesus is strong—he has no second thoughts in the garden and doesn't need anyone to carry his cross (19:17). Luke's Jesus is reliably compassionate and full of healing—only Luke tells us, for instance, that on the eve of the crucifixion, when one of the disciples cuts off the ear of the high priest's slave, Jesus pauses to heal the slave (22:51).

What's called Jesus' "cry of dereliction" occurs in Mark and Matthew. Indeed, it is the only "word from the cross" in these two accounts and indicates how fully human Jesus is and how completely he identifies with us. Some have said that because Jesus' prayer is taken from Psalm 22, it actually conveys Jesus' continued fidelity and confidence. But I suspect that Mark and Matthew were more interested in confessing to Christians who have themselves at times felt abandoned by God that they have a Lord and Savior that knows the depths of our sorrows and struggles . . . and understands them.

Phil Snider

Who is...
Phil Snider

*I refuse to buy cool emergent eyeglasses,
even though my glasses are so 2002.*

A. According to G. K. Chesterton, Jesus' words on the cross testify that Christianity is the only religion in which God, for an instant, became an atheist. Similar religious thinkers have taken this a step further by saying that the most radical implication of the doctrine of the incarnation (the belief that God became human) is that, upon the death of Christ, God dies. This perspective not only takes the incarnation quite seriously but also leads to the conclusion that Christianity is a properly atheistic religion.

This may sound absurd, but the idea behind such thinking is summarized by twentieth-century theologian Dietrich Bonhoeffer: "God lets himself be pushed out of the world on to the cross. He is weak and powerless in the world, and that is precisely the way, the only way, in which he is with us and helps us . . . Christ helps us, not by virtue of his omnipotence, but by virtue of his weakness and suffering." Here, the "God who is with us is the God who forsakes us . . . Before God and with God we live without God."[7]

Perhaps the subversive kernel of Christianity is that God doesn't run the world but instead dies to the world. This in turn allows human beings to exert radical freedom and responsibility for the sake of the world. After all, when human beings leave it to some "big other" to fix everything, they neglect the radical freedom and responsibility that God has already given them. Thus it can be said that God's death is necessary in order for God's transformative work to begin.

Chris Haw

A. It partly depends on which gospel you are drawing from. Given my answer on the gospels, it should come as no surprise that John does not write this into his story.

The literary device here is a *remez*, which hints at a larger meaning by using a small citation. So the reader is supposed to *read all of Psalm 22* as a background here. Chesterton sees that this is the one moment when even God became an atheist—and depending on how deep your philosophy can go,

---

7. Dietrich Bonhoeffer, *Letters and Papers from Prison* (New York: Touchstone, 1997), 360–61.

this is either rhetorical flourish, a citation of an otherwise hopeful Psalm, or profound engagement with the absence of God.

We all can admit that Jesus' hopefulness and enchantment with the world is at least more sublime and clear than the hopes of atheism. But Jesus' capacity for despair, atheism, and disenchantment also appears to me as more courageous and aggressive than the so-called new atheism—a philosophy that Eugene McCarraher considers, on some points, a mere acquiescence to the nihilism of global capitalism. After all, it is one thing to say "life is meaning-less" or "God is dead" from a well-funded professor seat or through over-wrought existentialist self-pity; it is another to declare it while being tortured to death when standing up for goodness and justice.

Like I said previously, the gospels appear to necessitate some kind of indirect relationship with God—like, being a "son" or "sent by" or "united with." It does not seem unreasonable therefore to imagine Jesus feeling this "sent" degrading into a confused "abandoned," especially in a moment of agonizing torture.

Sherri Emmons

Who is...
Sherri Emmons

I spent five years as part of the Baha'i community.

A. Jesus' cry on the cross is one of the most gut-wrenching parts of the Bible, and one of the most profound proofs of his humanity. He felt the same pain we feel and had the same doubts. This passage is a big part of the reason I stay in the Christian church because I know that Christ understands my pains, my mistakes, and my doubts. And if Jesus is a part of God, then God understands, too.

But of course God did not abandon Jesus, any more than God abandons us when we are experiencing pain and loss. Life always involves pain and loss, that's how we grow as human beings. And God is with us in our pain, through the love that we show to one another in bad times, following Jesus' example.

Jarrod McKenna

A. Wrenching against his tearing flesh to raise his chest for air, the breath that created the world now gasps under the brutality of good creation corrupted. Crowned only with the thorns of our shame, dressed only in the dignity that could not be gambled away, this strange naked flame burns alone on this desert bush between two failed revolutionaries.

As deep calls to deep, so Eloi cries to Eloi, "*Lama sabachthani!*" into the darkening silence of the sky. Piercing doubt sung out faithfully in the pain-riddled poetry of the twenty-second Psalm, hope and horror wrestle in the excruciating cries of a suffering God. Out of the same lamenting lips Jesus calls from the misery of our slavery and cries simultaneously God's scandalous response. The presence is only felt in the ground-shaking absence.

Flowing from the true temple's hands, feet, and side is the defeat of evil, the end of exile, the forgiveness of sins, and the *shekinah* glory that will flood the earth with the presence of peace. Women weep from a distance as God is in Christ reconciling the world to himself. Yet it seems that God is dead to God. How strange a coronation that crowns the returning King with crucifixion, announcing that the meek one has inherited the earth and reigns not with a sword but as the Suffering Servant of all.

Why did Jesus cry out "My God, my God, why have you forsaken me?" Such questions are best asked from awe-filled silence of contemplation from where we can see why the centurion in terrified wonder would whisper the words, "Surely, this man was the Son of God."

Scriptural References

Psalm 22; Isaiah 53; Matthew 27:27–56; Mark 15:16–41, 33–34;
 1 Corinthians 1:18–31; 2:2; 2 Corinthians 5:16–21

Suggested Additional Sources for Reading

- David Lose, *Making Sense of Scripture* (Augsburg Fortress Press, 2009).
- Enter the Bible: http://www.enterthebible.org.
- G. K. Chesterton, *Orthodoxy* (John Lane, 1909).
- Dietrich Bonhoeffer, *Letters and Papers from Prison* (Touchstone, 1997).
- Adam Kotsko, *Žižek and Theology* (T & T Clark, 2008).
- John Caputo and Gianni Vattimo, *After the Death of God* (Columbia Univ. Press, 2007).
- N. T. Wright, *Following Jesus: Biblical Reflections on Discipleship* (Eerdmans, 1995).
- Lee C. Camp, *Mere Discipleship* (Brazos Press, 2003).
- Brad Jersak and Michael Hardin, *Stricken by God?: Nonviolent Identification and the Victory of Christ* (Eerdmans, 2007).
- Martin Scorsese, director, *The Last Temptation of Christ* (Universal Films, 1988).
- Marcus J. Borg and John Dominic Crossan, *The Last Week: A Day-by-Day Account of Jesus' Final Week in Jerusalem* (HarperOne, 2006).

Suggested Questions for Further Discussion/Thought

1. Of what value is it to know that however abandoned you may feel, Jesus has also felt that way and understands?
2. If "Christ helps us, not by virtue of his omnipotence, but by virtue of his weakness and suffering" (as Bonhoeffer suggests), do you think Christ's influence on your life becomes less important or more important?
3. Can you think of times when people have used Christian beliefs as an excuse not to care for the world? Name some examples.
4. Have you ever been moved to tears by the horrific beauty of a love that would undergo the cross?

13. Why doesn't there seem to be any physical evidence of Jesus' life?

Phil Snider

A. Most scholars think that Jesus existed, but there is a bunch of speculation regarding the actual events that defined his life. There are several activities recorded in the Bible about Jesus that no one can ever prove took place, and none more so than Jesus' resurrection.

Some people want to try to prove the reality of the resurrection in the same way they might prove whether or not aliens exist. The idea is that the resurrection is an event that, given the proper technology, could be captured on film, empirically verified, and studied in a lab. Yet all four gospels resist this idea, precisely because the "truth" of the resurrection—and of Christianity in general—isn't the kind of truth that can be studied in a lab, no matter how much "evidence" one might have.

Indeed, the truth of Christianity resists such banal forms, for it is *experienced* in the wake of transformative events that change the very fabric of our lives, events that leave us holding on for dear life in search of that which we know not, all the while hoping and sighing and dreaming and weeping to be changed again and again, to live into the vision that captivates and consumes us. We catch glimpses of this vision in scripture's proclamation of the kingdom of God as embodied and announced by the figure of Jesus Christ—a spectral figure that, despite whatever physical evidence we might have of his life, continues to haunt, disturb, and call out to us (in both wonderful and terrifying ways), kind of like a very holy ghost that is never, yet always, enough.

David Lose

A. Up until a century ago, there was no physical evidence for the lives of the overwhelming majority of humanity. Apart from a few isolated memories that might be passed down through a family, most of the people who have walked the face of this earth—who have laughed and wept, dreamed and worked, loved and lost, live and died—have left nothing behind to prove, let alone validate, their existence. Nothing. Zilch. Nada.

There is something profoundly moving, I think, to recognize that in leaving no physical trace, Jesus identifies himself with the vast huddled masses of humanity and so also with us.

I know what you're thinking. "Yeah, but Jesus was famous. Shouldn't famous people leave a mark?" Except that the point of the gospels was precisely that Jesus wasn't famous, that he was neither a superhero nor a demigod. Rather, Jesus was *just like us*. Why? Because he came to be both *with* us and *for* us—to redeem us—even the most ordinary among us. It's hard to identify with a superhero, but it may be easier to identity with Jesus who, as Paul writes, "Though he was in the form of God, did not regard equality with God as something to be exploited, but emptied himself" (Philippians 2:6–7a).

According to the gospels, nobody—not even his disciples—really understood who Jesus was until after his death, resurrection, and ascension. God's most important work, Christians confess, was hidden in the ordinary, even unlikely events of the life and death of a common, first-century Jew. Maybe if they had known they would have saved something. Maybe that would make it easier for us today. But what would that prove: that Jesus lived? The gospels confess something much greater: that God loves all of us, even the most ordinary.

Tripp Fuller

Who is...
Tripp Fuller

I picked my son's name so his initials would be E. T.

A. Jesus was a marginal peasant Jew in the first century. To a historian, that is a really important point. We have physical evidence of very few people from the first century in general and that includes literate, affluent, and public figures! That we have as many texts about his life, a community whose existence would be unthinkable without the historical personality behind it at least existing, and evidence that the opponents of Christianity never challenged the actual existence of the historical person, Jesus is about the strongest proof that you can get.

What this doesn't mean is that everything that is said about Jesus in the gospels or by historians is necessarily, factually true. I believe the insights we gain through historical studies can help us better understand the life of Jesus and the gospel texts in their context but their accuracy or persuasiveness is not the foundation of faith.

A Christian shouldn't be scared of seeking the truth and attempting to give a more robust account of Jesus' life in light of new historical knowledge. Ultimately perfect historical knowledge about Jesus doesn't result in anything new. The individual today has the same possibilities of the people of the first century who encountered Jesus: to become a disciple and follow his life-giving way of being in the world or not.

Chris Haw

We have more evidence for Jesus' existence than we have for many other events and persons in antiquity. But, admittedly, this evidence is virtually *only* textual. If we are asking *why*, this is because the event was two thousand years ago. If we are asking, "Can we believe in an event that we have mostly only oral history for?" I am drawn to recall the first wry lines of Chesterton's autobiography:

"Bowing down in blind credulity, as is my custom, before mere authority and the tradition of the elders, superstitiously swallowing a story I could not test at the time by experiment or private judgment, I am firmly of opinion that I was born on the twenty-ninth of May, 1874." It seems Chesterton has recognized that, even for the firmest and most assumed events of life, we eventually will need to trust in witnesses.

Scriptural References

Luke 24:13–35; John 20:11–18; 1 Corinthians 2:1–9

Suggested Additional Sources for Reading

- David Lose, *Making Sense of the Christian Faith* (Augsburg Fortress Press, 2010).
- John Caputo, *What Would Jesus Deconstruct?* (Baker Academic, 2007).
- Peter Rollins, *How (Not) to Speak of God* (Paraclete Press, 2006).
- Søren Kierkegaard, *The Sickness Unto Death* (Princeton Univ. Press, 1941).
- Peter Rollins, "One Day I Hope to Believe in God," http://peterrollins.net/blog/?p=587.

Suggested Questions for Further Discussion/Thought

1. Why do you think we seek "evidence"? What do we hope that will provide? What would faith be if it depended on evidence?
2. What has been the most transformative experience of your life? Do you think it is connected to religion or Christianity?
3. Do you think it is possible to prove the existence of God? Why or why not?

Question

14. In Isaiah, Satan is referred to as the "Morning Star" and so is Jesus in Revelation. In 1 Peter, Satan is compared to a lion, and in Revelation, Jesus too is called a lion. Are these parallels intentional? Why?

L. Shannon Moore

Who is...
L. Shannon Moore

There are always cookies in my cookie jar.

A. Stars played an important role in the ancient world. Many cultures even worshiped stars, although the Torah (the first five books of the Bible and an important part of the Hebrew Scriptures) forbade the Israelites to do so. Even so, stars are used with regularity as simile in the Bible for both good and evil: Abraham's children will be too numerous to count, yet the wicked are like stars that have wandered from their courses.[8]

Satan mythically (but not biblically) fell from Heaven as a rebel angel, and was likely interpreted through the years as the fallen star or "Morning Star" referenced in Isaiah and Luke. Likewise, the lion is used throughout the scriptures alternatively as a symbol of strength and wickedness.[9]

That Jesus is compared to both a star and a lion in Revelation, the grand-daddy of apocalyptic literature, is telling. And yes, I do think the parallels are intentional.

Revelation is the, well, revelation-via-vision of a man of God named John who is exiled on an island because of his Christian beliefs. The book foretells the ultimate showdown between good (God through Jesus Christ) and evil (Satan), though not with the scary precision that many modern-day Christians would desire. The writing is rife with symbolism, and the fact that Jesus is compared to both a star and a lion, as Satan has been in other writings, only serves to underscore the theme of Revelation—that God will ultimately triumph, even over similes.

---

8. Geoffrey Wigoder, ed., "Stars and Constellations," in *Illustrated Dictionary and Concordance of the Bible* (Jerusalem: G. G. The Jerusalem Publishing House, 1986).

9. Dietrich Bonhoeffer, *Letters and Papers from Prison* (New York: Touchstone, 1997), 360.

Mark Van Steenwyk

A. These parallels are, I believe, entirely intentional. Satan is, in a way, the anti-Jesus. What does it mean to say that Jesus is the Morning Star and a lion? It means that he is a glorious ruler. He is God's glorious ruler. When such things are said of Satan, it means that Satan has set himself up as a glorious ruler—but his rule is illegitimate.

Before Jesus entered into his public ministry, he spent forty days in the wilderness being tempted by Satan. Satan offered him power—economic, political, and religious power, but Jesus refused. Jesus consistently refused to dominate people and, instead, sought to serve and liberate. Satan is all about domination.

Jesus and Satan offer two competing ways of living in the world. In their own ways, they are both triumphant lions . . . they are both glorious stars in the heavens. But while one uses power to oppress, the other uses it to liberate.

It is ironic that in the past two thousand years we have slowly redefined Jesus into something that is increasingly Satan-like. Which Morning Star do we want to follow? If we want to embrace economic, religious, and political power over others then we are following Satan, even if we think we are doing so in the name of Jesus Christ.

Scriptural References

Genesis 15:5; Exodus 20:3; Deuteronomy 5:8; Proverbs 28:15; 30:30; Isaiah 14:12; Luke 4:1–13; 1 Peter 5:8; Jude v. 13; Revelation 4:7; 5:5; 9:17; 10:3; 13:2; 22:16

Suggested Additional Sources for Reading

- Leonard Sweet and Frank Viola, *The Jesus Manifesto* (available at http://www.thejesusmanifesto.com).
- John Howard Yoder, *The Politics of Jesus* (Eerdmans, 1972).
- Shane Claiborne and Chris Haw, *Jesus for President* (Zondervan, 2008).
- Fyodor Dostoevsky, "The Grand Inquisitor," in *Brothers Karamazov* (Bantam Classics, 1984).

Suggested Questions for Further Discussion/Thought

1. Which structures in our society are the most oppressive? Does it seem strange to think of them as satanic?
2. What do you do with the reality that Christianity has a history of committing great evil in the name of Jesus?

Question

15. Aren't Jesus' miracles similar to other healings and miracles recorded outside the Jewish and Christian tradition?

Brandon Gilvin

Who is...
Brandon Gilvin

I have been kicked out of Canada.

A. Absolutely. The ancient Near East was full of stories of magicians and miracle workers, many Jewish, and many served as antecedents for the stories of Jesus. Prophets such as Elisha (2 Kings) and Isaiah performed a number of acts that Jesus' miracles evoke.

Stories of miracles by Jesus' contemporaries such as Honi the Circle Drawer also continue to draw attention from historical-Jesus scholars.

And of course, similar healing stories, miracles, and miraculous births are attributed to other religious figures (human and divine) from other traditions.

Such stories have a variety of meanings within the contexts of the communities that teach them. From my perspective, it is less important to compare stories of traditions, as if we could judge which one is the most historically accurate, than it is for us to be able to ask what the stories of Jesus healing others has to say for us as twenty-first century Christians. Whether or not Jesus was a first century magician or a Hippocratic practitioner is not as much as a concern for me—but how we follow Jesus' example by working for sustainable health, nutrition, HIV and AIDS prevention, and other important issues in struggling communities is.

Mark Van Steenwyk

Who is...
Mark Van Steenwyk

My two-year-old son has helped me with "dumpster diving."

A. There have always been stories of wonder workers. And while there were certainly folks claiming miraculous powers wandering around the Roman Empire around the time of Jesus, it wasn't all that common. Nevertheless, popular perception tends to reflect the sensibilities of Monty Python's *The Life of Brian* where there seemed to be a messiah around every corner.

But that wasn't really the case. Respected scholar Raymond E. Brown wrote, "One should be wary of the claim that Jesus was portrayed like the many other miracle-working teachers, Jewish and pagan, of his era. The idea that such a figure was a commonplace in the 1st century is largely a fiction. Jesus is remembered as combining teaching with miracles intimately related to his teaching and that combination may be unique."[10]

Some folks claimed to do miracles. Most of these folks did it for personal profit—to wow the crowds. And there were certainly many spiritual teachers. But Jesus is largely unique in the way that he combined his miracles with his message. He didn't do miracles so that the crowds could be amazed. Rather he did acts of power to liberate people from oppression. His miracles were intentional acts of service and liberation. In his miracles, he fed the hungry. He gave sight to the blind. He cast demons out of the oppressed. He was, in everything he said and did, a liberator.

Peter J. Walker

Yes. Miracles have occurred in cultures and religions throughout history (as theological "proof," miracles only make a case for universalism more compelling). The church often argues that its truth relies on the historical anomaly of Christ, using miracles as key evidence. That's why things like the Zeitgeist videos on YouTube go viral so quickly and cause so much damage: We talk about how Jesus is wholly unique among world religions, and then what? Hope someone doesn't Google *Horus, Krishna,* or *Siddhārtha Gautama*?

C. S. Lewis argued that Christianity's profound difference is in its *historical* reality: that all religions echo a similar metanarrative but only one is the "true myth," the rest are like reflections in a mirror. I'm not sure I would even go that far. When I married my wife, I chose to stop playing "what if" about other beautiful women. I made a choice to give myself to her and to trust her based on who I knew her to be—*not* based on a belief that no other women existed. Have I stopped finding other women attractive? Do I believe she is the only person in the world I could ever be happy with? I won't play naive. But we *know* each other, and we have committed to exclusively love one another.

I have committed to loving Christ, not because I think he is my only available option or because I think his *miracles* uniquely prove his truth or even because I find other religions less compelling. I remain in this

---

10. Raymond E. Brown, *An Introduction to New Testament Christology* (Mahwah, NJ: Paulist Press, 1994), 63.

relationship because I have the audacity to believe I *know* Christ. Rather than passive belief, faith is a miracle I choose to participate in.

Phil Snider

A. While the short answer to this question is yes, it's important to keep in mind that the people who wrote the gospels used the miracle stories about Jesus in order to talk about the way their lives changed as a result of following Jesus. One of the coolest things about these stories is the way they function on several different levels at once, both literally and figuratively.

For instance, Mark's gospel describes two stories that each feature Jesus restoring the sight of a blind man (Mark 8:22–26 and 10:46–52). Close readers of Mark will notice these stories working together as a frame that surrounds Jesus' journey to Jerusalem, the place where Jesus ultimately confronts the powers that be and loses his life as a result. By framing Jesus' journey with these stories, part of what Mark tells us is that if we have the courage to follow Jesus all the way to Jerusalem—by joining Jesus in order to confront oppressive powers that be, no matter the cost—then we too will have our sight restored.

Just as the earliest followers of Jesus experienced transformation when they confronted the powers that be, no matter the cost, the same can be said of modern day heroes like Martin Luther King Jr. and Oscar Romero. When they stood up to the powers that be on behalf of the oppressed—even though they ultimately lost their own lives as a result—we affirm that (1) they are representative of those who see most clearly and (2) if we follow Jesus the same way, we just might have our sight restored as well.

Scriptural References

2 Kings; Isaiah; Mark 8:11–12, 22–26, 27–30; 10:46–52; Luke 4:14–21; 5:14

Suggested Additional Sources for Reading

- David Rhoads, *Mark as Story* (Augsburg Fortress Press, 1999).
- Marcus Borg and John Dominic Crossan, *The Last Week: What the Gospels Really Teach about Jesus's Final Days in Jerusalem* (HarperOne, 2006).
- Raymond E. Brown, *An Introduction to New Testament Christology* (Paulist Press, 1994).
- Robert Funk, *The Acts of Jesus* (Polebridge Press, 1998).
- Graham Twelftree, *Jesus the Miracle Worker* (IVP Academic, 1999).
- *Wikipedia*, s.v. "Miracles of Jesus," http://en.wikipedia.org/wiki/Miracles_of_Jesus#List_of_miracles_in_the_four_Gospels.

- *Wikipedia*, s.v. "Jesus in Comparative Mythology," http://en.wikipedia.org/wiki/Jesus_Christ_in_comparative_mythology.
- C. S. Lewis, *Mere Christianity* (Macmillan, 1952).
- C. S. Lewis, *Out of the Silent Planet* (Macmillan, 1946).
- Peter Joseph, director, *Zeitgeist: Moving Forward* (Gentle Machine, 2011). DVD available at http://www.zeitgeistmovie.com.
- Amy-Jill Levine, Dale C. Allison, John Dominic Crossan, eds., *The Historical Jesus in Context* (Princeton Univ. Press, 2006).
- James H. Charlesworth, *The Historical Jesus: An Essential Guide* (Abingdon Press, 2008).

Suggested Questions for Further Discussion/Thought

1. What would it mean if there were other miracle workers in Jesus' day?
2. Is it important to believe that Jesus was actually able to do miracles?
3. Do I need miracles to believe?
4. Can I believe in what I have not seen?
5. Does my religious faith depend on its exclusive truth?
6. Are miracles in other religions from the same God, or are they dangerous illusions?
7. Consider the theological symbolism at work in stories about Jesus turning water into wine, multiplying the loaves and fishes, walking on water, and so on. How does this affect the meaning of each story?

uestion

16. The Bible says that Jesus had siblings. Does that mean that there are people alive today who are from his family's bloodline? Where are they? Who are they?

Pablo A. Jiménez

Who is...
Pablo A. Jiménez

I have played with salsa bands.

Yes, the Bible states clearly that Jesus had siblings. For example, John 7:3 affirms that Jesus had brothers, although they did not believe in him. Mark 3:31–35, Matthew 12:46–50 and Luke 8:19–21 also affirm that Jesus had siblings.

Matthew also affirms that Jesus had siblings named James, Joseph, Simon, and Judas, plus several sisters (Matthew 13:55–56). Interestingly, the Apostle Paul mentions a person named James, who is identified as "the Lord's brother" in Galatians 1:19. Paul also mentions James in Galatians 2:9 and 12. Acts also mentions James in 12:17, 15:13, and 21:18. It is believed that James either wrote or inspired the epistle of James. The epistle of Judas may also be either inspired or written by Judas, another one of Jesus' brothers.

The church tradition teaches us that James became the leader of the church in Jerusalem. History teaches us that James was assassinated during the turmoil that led to the Jewish War.

It is probable that Jesus' other siblings also died during the war. Some could have survived, meaning that there may be descendants of Christ among us. However, on the absence of Jesus' DNA, it would be utterly impossible to prove a genetic link.

What we do know is that the theory that Jesus married Mary Magdalene, who supposedly bore him a child that became the patriarch of European royal families, is not based on any believable evidence or proven facts.

Sherri Emmons

The Bible indeed says that Jesus had siblings. In Matthew 13:54–56, they are listed by name (at least the brothers are listed; the sisters, of course, are nameless): "Is not his mother called Mary? And are not his brothers James and Joseph and Simon and Judas? And are not all his sisters with us?"

We know that after the crucifixion, James was one of the leaders of the early Christian community, although his influenced waned as Paul's grew.

It only makes sense that at least some of Jesus' siblings had children and that there are people walking around today who share Jesus' bloodline. Even if we accept the virgin birth story, Mary's DNA would have been passed on to all her children. Who and where these descendants are doesn't matter, really, because it isn't Christ's DNA that we follow; it is his teaching.

Tripp Fuller

Since Jesus was Jewish we know that, broadly, there are people sharing his family's bloodline. Beyond that there is little histori-cal consensus past the recognition that Joseph had other children, probably with a wife before Mary. The most famous step or half brother is James who exercised a leadership role in the early church in the Jerusalem. Yet it is important to note that Jesus had his own way of defining his family.

In the gospel of Mark we hear a story of his family seeking him out while in a crowded house. When hears of this, the text says, "'Who are my mother and my brothers?' And looking at those who sat around him, he said, 'Here are my mother and my brothers! Whoever does the will of God is my brother and sister and mother.'" Jesus uses this moment as an opportunity to redefine what it means to be in his family; namely it means faithfulness to God. If for some reason we discovered the bloodline of Jesus or some artifact that con-tained the DNA of Jesus, we shouldn't expect it to be strikingly different.

What differentiated Jesus was not in the genes but in his living. The com-plete faithfulness of Jesus to the God he knew as *Abba* is what sets him apart on the human plane. Not only that but for Paul it is precisely his mind that we are to seek (Philippians 2:5) and it is Christ's faithfulness to God that saves us (Galatians 3:22). With that in mind, I think we can say with Jesus and Paul that there are indeed members of Christ's family alive today, and they are those who know and do the loving will of God in the world.

Scriptural References

Matthew 12:46–50; 13:54–56; Mark 3:31–35; 6:1–3; Luke 8:19–21; John 7:3; Acts 12:17; 15:13; 21:18; Galatians 1:19; 2:9; 12

Suggested Additional Sources for Reading

- Robert H. Eisenman, *James the Brother of Jesus: The Key to Unlocking the Secrets of Early Christianity and the Dead Sea Scrolls* (Viking Penguin, 1997).

Are there people alive who are from Jesus' family's bloodline?

- Jeffrey J. Bütz, *The Brother of Jesus and the Lost Teachings of Christianity* (Inner Traditions, 2005).
- John Painter, *Just James: The Brother of Jesus in History and Tradition* (Univ. of South Carolina Press, 2004).
- "Jesus' Family Tree," Frontline Web site, http://www.pbs.org/wgbh/pages/frontline/shows/religion/jesus/tree.html.

Suggested Questions for Further Discussion/Thought

1. What, if anything, would it mean for the church or your own faith to know that descendants of Jesus' bloodline were alive today?
2. Does it matter to you if Jesus married and had children? Why or why not?
3. Where do you think the story of Jesus marrying and having children came from?

17. When Jesus participates in the Last Supper, doesn't that mean he's eating his own body and drinking his own blood?

Becky Garrison

Who is...
Becky Garrison

I wrote my first piece when I was nine.

A. Christians differ widely as to how they interpret the Last Supper, ranging from transubstantiation—where the bread and wine become the body and blood of Christ—to a memorial that pays homage to Jesus' last night on earth. For liturgically minded Christians (Catholic, Orthodox, Anglican, Lutheran), the ritual of receiving the body and blood of Christ becomes a sacrament, a term that means "the outward expression of an inward act."

Most Protestants tend to place their emphasis on preaching, so one might find communion administered anywhere from biweekly to not at all. Regardless of the emphasis a given denomination places on this ritualistic act, no one in his or her right mind would call Christ a cannibal. That's just disgusting.

Mark Van Steenwyk

A. At the Last Supper, Jesus told his disciples that the bread and wine they were eating and drinking were his body and blood. Catholics traditionally believe that when you eat the bread and wine at mass, you're actually eating the flesh and blood of Jesus. Since the Last Supper was the first communion, or eucharist, I'd imagine that Jesus eating bread and drinking wine with his disciples poses an odd question: Did Jesus eat himself at the Last Supper?

Personally, since I am not a Catholic, I'm not confronted with the question of cannibalism. I believe that communion is, for the most part, symbolic. I think Jesus was engaging in a bit of performance art—telling his disciples that he was about to be killed and that his disciples should partake of a similar sort of death. In other words, this is a vivid way of telling his followers that they should "take up their crosses" and be willing to lay down their lives for the movement.

So when it comes to the question of cannibalism, I'm off the hook. However, I believe that Christ is indeed present in a flesh-and-blood way when we share communion with one another—but that is because we, the followers of Jesus Christ, are his body and blood. He is present in us whenever we break bread together in his name. And so, I suppose, if we were to eat each other, it would count as a double dose of cannibalism!

Sherri Emmons

A. OK, first . . . ewww! This is what happens when we take the Bible literally, and it's why so many people today get turned off by the church. Jesus broke bread and poured wine and passed them to his friends and said, "Take, eat, this is my body, this is my blood." Did any of his disciples gag? Did they refuse to take the elements? No, because they understood that Jesus was using metaphors.

We can understand it the same way when Jesus says in Matthew 13:31, "The kingdom of heaven is like a mustard seed that someone took and sowed in his field." Is the kingdom of heaven really like a mustard seed? If we eat mustard, are we devouring the kingdom of heaven? Of course not.

Jesus taught his followers using stories and images that they could understand—he was the shepherd tending his flock; he was the bridegroom and the church, his bride. We accept these metaphors for what they are. So why do we get hung up on the bread and wine as body and blood?

Scriptural References

Matthew 26; Mark 14; Luke 22; John 13

Suggested Additional Sources for Reading

- Henri Nouwen, *Can You Drink the Cup?* (Ave Maria Press, 1996).
- Sara Miles, *Take This Bread: A Radical Conversion* (Ballantine, 2008).
- John H. Armstrong, ed., *Understanding Four Views on the Lord's Supper* (Zondervan, 2007).
- Ben Witherington III, *Making a Meal of It: Rethinking the Theology of the Lord's Supper* (Baylor Univ. Press, 2008).
- Martin E. Marty, *The Lord's Supper* (Augsburg Fortress Press, 1964).

Suggested Questions for Further Discussion/Thought

1. What does it mean for you to receive the body and blood of Jesus Christ?
2. Do you think eating communion is important?
3. Why do you think Jesus made a point of eating a meal with his disciples before he was executed?

18. Mormons believe that Jesus appeared to thousands of North American natives. Why do so many other Christians not believe this happened?

Sherri Emmons

A. It's a question of Joseph Smith's legitimacy as a prophet. I have great respect for members of the Church of Jesus Christ of Latter-Day Saints. The folks I know who believe in the Book of Mormon are decent, thinking, hardworking people who are trying their best to live according to their beliefs.

That said, I don't believe Joseph Smith was a prophet. I think he was either misguided or a very good scam artist. His teachings on many things—from marriage to the afterlife—are so different from what we find in the Bible that everything he says about Jesus and his teachings is suspect.

God may, indeed, have appeared to the Native Americans, but I don't see any evidence anywhere that Christ visited them. I could be wrong, of course. But I have to base my beliefs on the book that makes sense to me, and that is the gospel.

Peter J. Walker

Who is...
Peter J. Walker

My best friend played "Hater Jesus" in an Everclear music video of the same name.

A. Lack of paleontological or archaeological evidence notwithstanding, the biggest problem with Mormon belief regarding Jesus' visit to North America is not its theological dissonance with mainstream Christendom. The trouble with saying that Jesus appeared to Native Americans is that it undermines and disregards what Native American tribes and cultures have to say about themselves. It's not unlike contemporary evangelical efforts to give Israelis and the modern state of Israel specifically Christian eschatological identities. When a dominant group (e.g., white, American, Christian) uses a marginalized community as a sort of "prop" in the narrative of its religious drama, it co-opts that culture and stifles its voice.

Conservative evangelicals vehemently "support" Israel, but they ultimately tend to believe Israelis are doomed to hell unless they convert. They're made a plot point for the Christian apocalypse. Mormons believe the Native Americans (Lamanites) were rogue Israelites, cursed with dark skin. Later they were visited by Jesus and initially converted, but soon rejected Christianity. Theirs is a cautionary tale comprising cultural caricatures and an erroneous history of the Lamanite extermination of their light-skinned neighbors, the Nephites.

But the historicity of this issue is less important to me than the ultimate impact such belief has on an already-marginalized people group. In an increasingly pluralistic world, it is more important than ever for us to pay attention to the traditions of our neighbors and honor the stories they tell. Some (not all) tribal narratives contain unique messianic stories of their own, but those do not easily serve the often-exploitive purposes of western Christians.

Suggested Additional Sources for Reading

- Richard Twiss, *One Church, Many Tribes: Following Jesus the Way God Made You* (Regal, 2000).
- Randy Woodley, *Living in Color: Embracing God's Passion for Ethnic Diversity* (IVP, 2004).
- Ched Myers, *Who Will Roll Away the Stone?: Discipleship Queries for First World Christians* (Orbis, 1994).
- Wiconi International: http://www.wiconi.com.
- Anne Cameron, *Daughters of Copper Woman* (Press Gang, 1981).
- "All about the Mormons," *South Park* season 7, episode 12.
- Joseph Smith Jr., *The Book of Mormon: Another Testament of Jesus Christ*.
- Richard Lyman Bushman, *Joseph Smith: Rough Stone Rolling* (Vintage, 2007).
- Jon Krakauer, *Under the Banner of Heaven: A Story of Violent Faith* (Anchor, 2004).

Suggested Questions for Further Discussion/Thought

1. Have you ever been mischaracterized by others? Has your family or your church?
2. What do you know about the Mormon faith? Upon what do you base your opinions about it?
3. Would it change your faith if you learned that all the teachings in Mormonism were true? If so, how?

19. What's the big deal with the Shroud of Turin? Is it real or fake? If it's fake, why create it in the first place?

David Lose

A. The most studied artifact in human history, the Shroud of Turin is a linen cloth bearing the image of a man who looks to have suffered torture, perhaps crucifixion. Lots of people believe that man may have been Jesus of Nazareth, and that the shroud is the cloth in which his body was wrapped. And lots of people don't believe it, instead concluding that the shroud probably originated in the Middle Ages, perhaps either covering someone else who had been crucified or produced as a fake. Debate rages about whether the shroud—and face—could possibly belong to Jesus. Given most of the scientific evidence, including carbon testing on part of the fabric, I suspect it's not.

What's the big deal? Great question. In the Middle Ages, relics connected to Jesus and the earliest Christians were highly valued for two reasons: They were often believed to possess healing properties, the power of the original owner apparently rubbing off onto the object, and they conveyed spiritual blessings, in particular reducing the amount of time one spent in purgatory (sort of the holding place between heaven and hell where heaven-destined Christians worked off their remaining sins after death).

More recently, people may venerate the shroud because they think that it is a tangible memorial to Jesus and that it provides physical evidence corroborating the gospel stories about Jesus.

If it's fake, I suppose those who produced it hoped to cash in on any or all the reasons mentioned previously, or perhaps they merely wanted to attract crowds. I couldn't give a hoot whether it's real or not. Evidence that a man existed doesn't assure us that he was what he and others claimed: God's Son, the living Word, love incarnate. That still needs to be taken on faith.

Becky Garrison

A. During the crusades a market developed to peddle holy artifacts, a practice that continues today in Israel. For those who could not make the trek to Jerusalem to walk in the Savior's steps, they could still touch a piece of holy history.

Among the thousands of artifacts that one finds ensconced in cathedrals and museums throughout Europe, the shroud stands alone as being the most famous of the holies of holies. Nina Burleigh, author of *Unholy Business: A True Tale of Faith, Greed and Forgery in the Holy Land*, offers a succinct description of the history of the Shroud of Turin: "It is said to have come from Jerusalem, possibly brought over by the Knights Templar, a monastic Christian fighting sect formed to protect pilgrims to the Holy Land in the twelfth century."[11]

As reported by Peter Manseau on *Religion Dispatches*,[12] ever since Turinese photographer Secondo Pia received permission to create glass-plate renderings of a tattered piece of cloth in a local church, pictures of the Shroud of Turin, the supposed burial cloth of Jesus Christ—have been reproduced around the world, turning up every few years like crime scene photos from the coldest of cases.

Even the Catholic Church admits that the shroud is biblically bogus. To quote Cardinal Giovanni Saldarini, former Archbishop of Turin, "The Shroud is not Christ but a reminder of him."

Sherri Emmons

I'm not sure who created the Shroud of Turin, but I'm pretty sure it's a fake. It's a fascinating relic, and I would love to know how someone in the Middle Ages could have pulled it off.

In 1988, the Vatican allowed researchers from three independent sources—Oxford University, the University of Arizona, and the Swiss Federal Institute of Technology—to take small samples of the linen many believe is the burial shroud of Jesus. These samples were tested using carbon dating in three different locations. Each research team came to the same conclusion. The cloth originated in medieval times—somewhere around the middle of the fourteenth century. This was a time when religious relics were sold all over Europe—everything from bone shards of John the Baptist to pieces of the cross. The creators of these relics made good money off them, and I am pretty sure the Shroud of Turin falls into this class.

Suggested Additional Source for Reading

- Nina Burleigh, *Unholy Business: A True Tale of Faith, Greed and Forgery in the Holy Land* (Smithsonian/Collins, 2008).

Suggested Questions for Further Discussion/Thought

1. Why do we need ontological proof in order to believe?
2. Why do these physical objects hold such enduring spiritual fascination?

---

11. Nina Burleigh, "Science and Belief in Turin," *Huffington Post*, April 11, 2010.

12. Peter Manseau, "Jesus in 3-D: The Shroud of Turin Meets the 21st Century," *Religion Dispatches*, April 6, 2010.

20. Why did Jesus instruct people at times not to tell others who he was? Wasn't this contrary to the idea of spreading the good news of his presence on earth?

Lee C. Camp

Who is...
Lee C. Camp

I grew up in Talladega, Alabama.

A. The gospel of Mark particularly highlights the "messianic secret," in which the demons or those healed by Jesus should not go about proclaiming that Jesus was the Messiah. Perhaps even more troubling, the gospel of Mark reports that, in response to Peter's proclamation that he believed Jesus to be the Messiah, Jesus sharply tells Peter to keep quiet about it. And the unfolding narrative in Mark 8–10 indicates that it is precisely those who are so sure they know who Jesus is who so sorely misunderstand him.

What sense could this make, when we believe "Jesus is Messiah" is the message that should be proclaimed to the entire world, and yet we have Jesus telling the disciples to keep quiet about it? It actually makes much sense when we see that Jesus is interested in more than mere repetition of orthodox words; he is more concerned with right practice and understanding. "Savior" and "Messiah," for many in Jesus' day, connoted bearing the sword against the enemies of God. Yet Jesus chose a different way, that of Suffering Servanthood as opposed to sword-bearing Savior. To say, "Jesus is Messiah" meant, for many—as it would come to mean for crusaders killing Muslims, or for Puritans killing Native Americans—that the perceived enemies of God could be slaughtered in the name of righteousness.

But it has become common wisdom that the Jews misunderstood Jesus; we Christians believe that Jesus did not come to establish a kingdom on earth, but to allow us to go to heaven when we die. But this misunderstands the misunderstanding. The synoptic gospels repeatedly proclaim that Jesus came to establish a kingdom—but one marked by nonviolent, suffering love. The kingdoms of this world reject this way, including the many nations that are called "Christian." Maybe Jesus would tell us to keep quiet, too.

Phil Snider

At first glance, it seems strange that Jesus would do remarkable things and then tell others to keep it all on the down-low, but as it turns out, there is actually a very cool reason this dynamic takes place. For the most part, these questions are related to what scholars call "Mark's messianic secret," which basically says that in Mark's gospel—which was very influential on the gospels that were later written by Matthew and Luke—the fullness of Jesus' identity as the Son of God can't be disclosed until the time of his crucifixion.

It's not because Jesus couldn't do wonderful things before this time but rather because the gospel writers wanted people to know that the kind of God revealed in Jesus is much more concerned with love, compassion, and vulnerability (as witnessed in the crucifixion) than with mind-boggling displays of power (as witnessed in miracles). After all, in the ancient world, several leaders claimed to have divine status, proclaiming themselves to be "sons of God." But virtually all of these folks—in stark contrast to Jesus—used their divine appeal in order to exploit others for personal gain.

That's why, in Christianity, the risen Christ is also the crucified one, for the revelation of God disclosed in Jesus Christ is one in which love always qualifies power, and not the other way around. As such, Mark's messianic secret represents a creative way of making this point.

Joan Ball

Who is...
Joan Ball

I used to sell the New York Post on the Verrazano Narrow Bridge (on the Brooklyn side).

I believe Jesus told people who he was when his ministry and the glory of God were served by doing so. The scriptures reflect a Jesus that was, among many other things, devout in his desire to hear and follow the will of the Father. He frequently separated himself from the masses (and their needs) to pray and confirm his intention to fulfill his calling at all costs.

This was evident from the outset of his public ministry when he expressed mild frustration with Mary for pointing out that they were out of wine at the wedding in Cana. "Woman, what concern is that to you and to me?" he says in John 2:4. "My hour has not yet come."

73

I view this exchange as a bellwether of his desire to serve the people with whom he spent his days, but only when it served what he discerned to be the broader will of the Father. Of course, knowing the end from the beginning, he could rest assured that the good news would be spread eventually.

Scriptural References

Mark 8–10; 9:30–32; 15:39; John 17:6–9; 1 Corinthians 15

Suggested Additional Sources for Reading

- C. M. Tuckett, "Messianic Secret," in *The Anchor Bible Dictionary IV*, 797–800.
- Thomas Merton, *No Man Is an Island* (Harcourt, Brace, 1955).

Suggested Questions for Further Discussion/Thought

1. What are ways you suspect that we—like the disciples in the gospel of Mark—might misunderstand what it means for Jesus to be Messiah?
2. Which characteristics of God are most important for you (power, might, love, grace, etc.)? Why?
3. If you were a Christian missionary responsible for spreading the good news, how might Jesus' revelation of God's love affect your message? Would it lead you to be more condemning of others or more affirming of others?
4. Have you ever thought about God's revelation in terms of vulnerability or weakness? How might such a perspective influence the kind of God that we worship?

Question

21. Did Jesus understand himself to be God, like God, in line with God, or something else? Did he understand this from birth? If not, then when did he begin to understand it and how?

Becky Garrison

Now we come to one of those questions that has caused way too many faith fistfights. In a nutshell, we can't answer that question definitively. According to the gospel of John, Jesus knew he was God from the beginning of time. Matthew and Mark cite the revelation of Jesus as the Messiah at the moment when he was baptized by John, while Luke points to the beginning when the boy Jesus was hanging out, doing his Father's business.

But one thing is clear—by the time Jesus set out for Jerusalem, he knew without a doubt that his kingdom was not of this world and that he was going to be crucified before rising from the dead.

R. M. Keelan Downton

Who is...
R. M. Keelan Downton
I type using a Dvorak keyboard layout.

If you start from a belief that Jesus came to convey a set of facts, it's pretty puzzling that there's not a checklist somewhere. If the purpose of reading the gospels is to piece together such a checklist, it is immensely important that Jesus have access to the complete knowledge of God (omniscience, if you want the jargon)—probably from puberty but at least from the beginning of his public ministry.

You need to be able to trust that each incident and phrase was carefully planned to communicate some part of that total knowledge, not the result of Jesus struggling like us to make decisions in a world of uncertain outcomes. But this makes Jesus otherworldly and disconnected from the everyday problems of life in a way that is not supported by the gospel narratives.

If, on the other hand, you start from an assertion that Jesus came to proclaim and enact the true order of the world, the first question is not "how did Jesus think about himself?" but "does Jesus reveal God?" The complete answer to this second question can only be seen from the other side of the resurrection: the way that Jesus reveals God demonstrates that Jesus, as Messiah and Christ, must be God.

L. Shannon Moore

Who is...
L. Shannon Moore

I went through the entire fifth grade as "Shane" because I was afraid to tell my teacher he had written my name down wrong on my desk.

A. I'll answer this backward. Based on the only biblical account pertaining to Jesus' boyhood, I think he always knew he had a special purpose. Separated from his parents, and later found in the temple having a discussion with the teachers, Jesus' reply in Luke 2 to his mother's scolding is, "I must be in my Father's house."

I don't think, however, that Jesus knew the importance of what God had in store for him until his baptism. In three books of the Bible, we read that after Jesus is baptized, the heavens open, the Spirit of God descends upon him, and a voice from heaven (presumably God's) declares him to be the "beloved Son." Talk about pressure.

And so it seems that throughout the gospels, Jesus sees himself as just that—God's beloved Son, sent to help people better understand God by forgiving their sins, healing the sick, and advocating justice for the poor. He prayed *to* God and preached *about* God, but did not consider himself to *be* God.

One of the main reasons that people attribute divinity to Jesus is because of the miracles that he performed. But Jesus kind of explains this in Matthew 17 when he says, "If you have faith and do not doubt . . . if you say to this mountain, 'Be lifted up and thrown into the sea,' it will be done." And that's the way I see it—Jesus saw himself as a human, sent from God, and gifted with the ability to do extraordinary things because *he did not doubt.*

Chris Haw

A. It depends on which gospel you ask. The synoptic gospels (Matthew, Mark, Luke) all share a type of Jesus—no doubt with some variations—whose humanity is more emphasized than the Jesus in John. While the synoptics certainly have their colors of divinity mixed in,

John's Jesus easily foretells events, can see beyond where his body is, and seems in charge of even his own arrest and death.

But even the highest Johannine proclamations from Jesus' mouth still involve some kind of mediation and indirection. John Robinson, in *Honest to God*, puts it something like this: "Jesus never says directly, 'I am God.' Rather, everything has some kind of differentiation, like 'if you have seen me, you have seen God' or 'I and the Father are One,' or 'the Father sent me,' etc." Jesus doesn't say, "I am the Father" rather he is sent from the Father, has seen him, is united with him, and so on.

Perhaps even more interestingly, what do we even mean by "God"? N. T. Wright also takes this up this quite well in his book *Jesus and the Victory of God* by asking what the word *God* meant, particularly in Jesus' day. Jesus is a fantastic instance to ask, "[J]udging from him, what is God and what is humanity?" For, in this person, we see both redefined.

"God," whatever that means, is something or someone who would love us, forgive us for our murderous evils, teach us, heal us, and submit to being crucified by us. And a "human," whatever that means, is someone who can live in union with God or reveal the very being of God.

Amy Reeder Worley

Who is...
Amy Reeder Worley

I practice yoga. I don't do yoga.

A. I was raised in a southern, fundamentalist Christian church and taught that Jesus is both *the Son of* God and *is* God. When I asked how Jesus could be human *and* God, I got an unsatisfying shtick about a house—God was a house and Jesus was a room in that house. They were the same but different. That metaphor only frustrated me.

I spent years divorced from Christianity because I could not intellectually conceive of Jesus' relationship to God in this way. Surprisingly it was my foray into Buddhism and Yoga that motivated me to rethink the "God language" I learned as a child.

Jesus articulates how he viewed himself in relation to God in Luke. Jesus, quoting Isaiah, says, "The spirit of the Lord is *on me*, because he *has anointed* me to preach good news to the poor. He has sent me to proclaim freedom for the prisoners, and recovery of sight for the blind, and to set the oppressed free" (Luke 4:18, NIV).

As a child, I had been told Jesus' divinity was like a math problem. Divine = God. Thus Human Jesus + Divinity = God. But divine also means "of, relating to, emanating from, or being the expression of" God. My practice of Yoga taught that spiritual seekers strive to "yoke" or "bring together" humankind and God. Informed by my yogic and Buddhist reading, I came to understand that Jesus viewed himself as being *anointed by* God—*that is,* yoked with the sacred.

Through prayer, submission, and devaluing material things (also Buddhist concepts) Jesus, acting *of* or *in* God, worked for justice and sought to heal those "blind" to God's ways. The hope in this Christology is that by following the way of Jesus we too can yoke ourselves with the sacred.

Scriptural References

Matthew 3:16–17; Mark 1:10–11; 6:45; Luke 2:41–52; 3:21–22; 4:18; 21:21; 22:42; John 1:1–5; Acts 17:28

Suggested Additional Sources for Reading

- Marcus Borg and N. T. Wright, *Meaning of Jesus: Two Visions* (HarperOne, 2007).
- Patanjali, *The Yoga Sutras*, trans. Edwin F. Bryant (North Point Press, 2009).
- Thich Nat Hanh, *Living Buddha, Living Christ* (Riverhead, 1995).
- Marcus Borg, *Jesus and Buddha: The Parallel Sayings* (Ulysses Press, 1997).
- Paul Knitter, *Without Buddha I Could Not Be a Christian* (Oneworld, 2009).
- Thomas Merton, *New Seeds of Contemplation* (New Directions, 1961).
- John A. T. Robinson, *Honest to God* (SCM, 1963).
- N. T. Wright, *The Challenge of Jesus* (InterVarsity Press, 1999), especially chapter 5.

Suggested Questions for Further Discussion/Thought

1. Why can't the gospel writers come to a consensus regarding the moment Jesus of Nazareth knew he was Christ, the Messiah, and Son of God?
2. Is it important to believe that Jesus is God?
3. Could you be a Christian if you knew without a doubt that Jesus was not divine?
4. Are there any God terms that you may need to rethink or redefine?
5. Do you believe that God is "out there" somewhere, as opposed to a force within and of the world?
6. What can you discern in the Bible about the early churches' view of Jesus' relationship to God? How is it similar or different from your view?

uestion

22. Is it possible that Jesus married and had children?

Christian Piatt

Who is...
Christian Piatt

I once had a job cleaning out condemned apartment buildings.

A. It's certainly possible. There have been theories about this for centuries, but interest in Jesus' direct bloodline has exploded since the *Da Vinci Code* novel brought the Merovingians into popular consciousness.

Though there is no record of Jesus marrying or having children, there are historical myths that a sect of the Merovingians secretly protects the direct bloodline of Christ. It's an intriguing concept, but again, there's no actual evidence.

More interesting to me is why some people feel so strongly that they must argue that Jesus *didn't* marry or have kids. More specifically, the issue seems to focus on the problem some people have with the possibility that Jesus ever had sex.

The western, Puritanical consensus around sex generally is that it's inherently dirty or sinful. And of course, there is plenty of material in the Bible that can support this attitude, such as Adam and Eve being made aware (i.e., ashamed) of their nakedness, and the very idea that Jesus was born of a virgin.

From one perspective, the Immaculate Conception makes room for God's direct intervention into the beginning of Jesus' life. But seen another way, it removes the actual act of sex from his creation. This makes it easy for us to lay our judgments about sex onto the Christian faith.

Of course, this attitude is hard to reconcile with other sacred texts, such as the Song of Songs, which celebrates sexuality and the act of sex itself as a wonderfully integral part of the human spiritual experience.

So was Jesus any more or less human or divine if he had sex? Our answers to this seem to tell us much more about ourselves and our own attitudes about sex than it does about Jesus.

Peter J. Walker

A. Making absolute statements about someone who lived two thousand years ago is unavoidably perilous. Still, a host of ancient writings more or less affirms the gospel accounts of Jesus' celibate

79

life. Only a few extant texts—most of them more historically questionable than their canonical counterparts—argue otherwise. But I'm no archaeologist or scholar. Rather I want to address the cultural landscape on which this question arises.

Christianity habitually adopts all-or-nothing "political platforms" that set themselves up for implosion if one tenet is determined untrue. So every time we discover that the earth is round, or the universe is older than five thousand years, or women are people, or sexuality isn't "chosen," the first response is denial, the second response is loss of faith (by untold thousands), and the final response is eventually adaptation or accommodation. But by the time Christianity adapts to new paradigms, the rest of the world is far ahead of us—so much so that they stopped caring about what we were arguing over, long ago. And we wonder why our "good news" seems so stodgy and lifeless. We keep fighting the wrong battles, taking our eyes off the liberating mission of Jesus' *new kind of humanity.*

So here's my question in response: If we're wrong about Jesus, and he did marry and have children, does it change the truth? I'm not saying I believe that. I'm saying I'm prepared to adapt and keep my faith if I discover we are wrong. The survival of my relationship with Jesus is more important to me than the survival of my Christian orthodoxy. That's a matter of choice, as all matters of faith tend to be.

L. Shannon Moore

A. I guess anything is *possible*. But I don't think the idea that Jesus married and had children is *probable*.

Despite what we've heard and read in recent years from novelists, dreamers, and conspiracy theorists, nothing in the Bible indicates that Jesus was married or had any children. Now while I certainly don't believe that every detail of Jesus' life is described in the scriptures, it stands to reason that something as important as a spouse and kids would have merited at least a mention.

And contrary to popular belief, Jesus did not focus on the family. He said that his teaching would bring division to households and that we should love God more than our families. Accordingly, Jesus didn't seem particularly attached to his family. In three of the gospels, he basically "disses" his mom and siblings (who are outside waiting to see him), saying, "Who is my mother, and who are my brothers? . . . whoever does the will of my Father in heaven is my brother and sister and mother" (Matthew 12:48–50). Harsh!

Jesus focused on fulfilling his destiny as the Messiah, the Savior of his people. Quoting the ancient prophet Isaiah, he said as much in the synagogue in his hometown: "The Spirit of the Lord is upon me . . . he has anointed me to bring good news to the poor . . . to proclaim release to the captives . . . to let the oppressed go free" (Luke 4:18). All that might be difficult to achieve if you're trying to keep the wife happy and the kids fed.

Scriptural References

Genesis 3; Song of Solomon; Matthew 1; 10:34–36; 12:46–50; Mark 3:31–35; Luke 1; 12:49–56; 4:18, 8:19–21

Suggested Additional Sources for Reading

- Brandon Gilvin, *Solving the Da Vinci Code Mystery* (Chalice Press, 2004).
- Michael Baigent, Richard Leigh, and Henry Lincoln, *Holy Blood, Holy Grail: The Secret History of Jesus, the Shocking Legacy of the Grail* (Delacorte Press, 1982).
- James D. Tabor, *The Jesus Dynasty: The Hidden History of Jesus, His Royal Family, and the Birth of Christianity* (Simon and Schuster, 2006).
- Marcus J. Borg, *Meeting Jesus Again for the First Time: The Historical Jesus and the Heart of Contemporary Faith* (HarperSanFrancisco, 1994).

Suggested Questions for Further Discussion/Thought

1. Does it matter to you if Jesus married or had children? Why?
2. How have you seen theories about this, made popular in books and film, affect the attitudes of both Christians and non-Christians toward Jesus' humanity?
3. Does faith mean certainty?
4. Is my only choice for belief between *all* and *nothing*?
5. Shannon indicates that Jesus' attitude toward the family is harsh. Do you agree that we should love God more than our families? How many people do you think have the desire or ability to love God in this way?
6. If Jesus had married and had children, would his children have inherited any of his divine nature?

23. If Jesus could resurrect people, why didn't he do it more often?

Brandon Gilvin

Who is...
Brandon Gilvin

I have a thing for pad Thai.

A. The first thing to remember is that resurrection is not the same thing as resuscitation.

To resuscitate a body is to revive it—whether the cause is medical or miracle, one who is physically dead regains breath, mental capacity, and use of his or her faculties.

Resurrection is something else. The early disciples experienced Jesus' presence following his death in very powerful, "real" ways. Whether or not the resurrection was the actual resuscitation of Jesus' body can never be historically verified.

The resurrection of Jesus took on many meanings for the early Jesus movement—the great love of God for humanity and God's sovereignty over death and the political forces of death. Resurrection is more of a theological concept than a physical act.

For contemporary Christians, to say we believe in the resurrection does not necessarily mean that we believe that rotting human bodies can be reanimated (either now or in the first century), but our shared conviction that despite the realities of death, sickness, poverty, and oppression there is always hope for healing, health, and reconciliation and that it is core to Christian practice to help make such hope reality.

The stories of Jesus (and the apostles in Acts) performing resurrections point readers to choose peace in the face of violence, hope in the face of despair, and life in the face of death.

Christian Piatt

A. Stories of healing and raising the dead in scripture seem to raise more questions than they answer. And the raising of Lazarus in the gospel of John is perhaps the best known of these.

Why did Jesus pick Lazarus? Why not someone else, perhaps an innocent child? Why did he let Lazarus die in the first place? Why not intervene before he died? And is it some kind of cruel joke that Lazarus ultimately will have to die all over again? If you think about it, there's nothing that ever said those fed by Jesus never hungered again, or those healed of disease never got sick after that.

So are these miracles, such as the one involving Lazarus, just a selfish demonstration of power by Jesus? Was he showing favoritism? Did he care less about those he didn't save from suffering?

It helps to consider *why* the miracle stories are included throughout the gospels, namely to point in a particular direction where Jesus is leading throughout his ministry. Considered from a literary perspective, the story of Lazarus' resurrection parallels that of Jesus' resurrection in a number of ways. And by including this toward the end of Jesus' ministry on earth, the author is offering a foreshadowing of the death-conquering power expressed by Christ's love for humanity.

Jesus acknowledged that suffering was an inevitable byproduct of physical life. But the miracle stories provide at least small windows through which we can see a way out of the suffering, toward an existence in perfect communion with God, casting aside the struggles and hardships of this world, like so many rags left behind by Lazarus at the tomb.

That is the *real* life-giving message of the gospels.

Joan Ball

Who is...
Joan Ball

I was a ribbon-winning cattle judger in 4H as a kid.

A. This is such an "if I were God, this is how I would do it" kind of question. Forget why Jesus didn't resurrect people more often. Why is there death at all? Why hunger? Why do we get thirsty? Wouldn't it have been better to design the human body without the need for fuel and eliminate the need for food and drink altogether? Why is the sky blue? Are we there yet?

Eventually our questions about God are so similar to those children ask about the world around them that, if we are humble, we will begin to see that part of having faith in God is recognizing that there are questions for which we will never have answers. His ways are not our ways, which makes understanding God's thoughts challenging, if not impossible, for us. We are operating on a different set of assumptions and, in our arrogance, we frequently attempt to have God shift to our assumptions rather than conforming ourselves to God's.

If Jesus could resurrect people, why didn't he do it more often?

Scriptural References

Isaiah 55:8–9; Mark 16:1–8; John 11:1–46; Acts 9:36–43; Philippians 2:6–11; Colossians

Suggested Additional Sources for Reading

- J. N. D. Kelly, *Early Christian Doctrines* (A. & C. Black, 1958).
- Henry Chadwick, *The Early Church* (Hodder & Stoughton, 1968).
- Justo Gonzalez, *The Story of Christianity*, vol. 1 (HarperOne, 2010).
- Karen Armstrong, *A History of God* (Ballantine, 1994).
- Esther de Waal, *Living with Contradiction: An Introduction to Benedictine Spirituality* (Morehouse, 1998).
- Emmet Fox, *The Sermon on the Mount* (HarperOne, 1989).

Suggested Questions for Further Discussion/Thought

1. Which is more important: the actual miracles Jesus was said to have performed or the message they seem to convey?
2. What do you believe was the main reason for resurrections performed in scripture?

24. Galatians 3:22: Is it the faith of Jesus or faith in Jesus that's the key?

Amy Reeder Worley

A. It is *both* the faith *of* and *in* Jesus that lead to salvation, which is another word for "liberation."

Jesus' faith in God was absolute. He lived in complete service to God. Jesus prayed at Gethsemane (Matthew 26:36), after healing Simon's mother-in-law (Mark 1:35), before he was baptized (Luke 3:21), when the disciples asked him how to pray (Luke 11:1), before the transfiguration (Luke 9:28), before he was arrested (John 17: 1–26), and minutes before he died (Luke 23:46). Jesus' relationship with God was so intimate he called God "Abba," or daddy. He praised God's works (Luke 10:21). And he beseeched God to forgive his executioners (Luke 23:34).

Yet Jesus did not tell us to just have greater faith in God. Rather Jesus said he was the "light of the world. Whoever follows me will never walk in darkness but will have the light of life" (John 8:12). What did he mean? Jesus explained further, "I came from God and now I am here. I did not come on my own, but he sent me" (John 8:42), and "I know him and I keep his word" (John 8:55). In other words, come with me; I can illuminate for you a path to God.

In saying that faith in Jesus and the faith of Jesus are both "the key," we get dangerously close to a tautology (using different words to say the same thing). But in this case I don't mean that both Jesus' faith and faith in Jesus are the same. I mean that our faith in Jesus illuminates how to practice a faith that brings us closer to God.

Modern Christians focus so much on *believing*. We too often forget that faith requires practice, doing. Jesus embodied this practice. Our faith in Jesus as our guide to a relationship with God is a condition precedent to salvation or a liberating faith in God.

Pablo A. Jiménez

Who is...
Pablo A. Jiménez

I served as a missionary in Costa Rica from 1986 to 1988.

A. I have always preferred to speak about the faith of Jesus than about faith in Christ. Most people find this shocking and many have tried to correct my theological statements. However, I persist in speaking about the faith of Jesus.

In English, the phrase "the faith of Jesus" is ambiguous. It can mean "the faith that Jesus had," "the faith inspired by Jesus, who is our theological center," or "the faith that belongs to Jesus." When asked about which meaning I imply in my preaching, my answer is "Yes, I mean all of the above."

First, the Christian faith exists because Jesus was faithful to God and to the mission that God delegated on him. In this sense, the church exists because Jesus had *faith*, a term better understood as faithfulness and commitment.

Second, believers must see Jesus as the model of belief, conduct, and practice. We must strive to imitate Jesus' faith.

Third, believers belong to Jesus. This is what the phrase "Jesus is Lord" means, after all.

Of course, correctly understood, the phrase "to have faith in Jesus" implies all the theological ideas expressed previously. However, I have found that many understand it as simply acknowledging Jesus' existence, without a clear commitment of faith.

Therefore, for me sharing in the faith of Jesus is more important than having faith "in" him.

Christian Piatt

Who is...
Christian Piatt

In college, I was the lead singer for several rock bands and had hair down to my waist.

I would tend to say it depends on whom you ask, but based on my personal experience, maybe it has more to do with *when* you ask someone such a question about their understanding of Jesus.

I grew up understanding that the latter was the cornerstone of my faith, and ultimately, my salvation. This leaned heavily on the idea that acceptance of Jesus as Savior was the one and only way to heaven and that Jesus died for my sins.

I have since come to understand both this passage in Galatians, as well as the notions of atonement, salvation, and the place of Jesus in my faith, a little differently. Instead of Jesus dying *for* my sins, I now tend to embrace the concept that Jesus died *because* of our collective sinfulness, meaning that Jesus made himself fully vulnerable to the fearful, violent smallness that humanity brought to the cross to the point of death.

Why? Because Jesus believed in what God anointed, enlightened, and blessed him to do, more than life itself. That is, he claimed love as paramount over all else, including his own personal well-being.

This brings us to the idea of the faith of Jesus raised in the question. How could someone put his or her humanity aside in the name of such sacrificial love? To me, it would take divine inspiration to hold so fast to one's faith. And that same divine breath is what is passed on through the generations, within the body of Christ, as well as among those who embrace the spirit of Christ.

We've all heard the phrase "God is love," but for me, the point that Jesus endeavored to make, to the foot of Calvary and beyond the open mouth of the tomb, is that *love is God*.

Scriptural References

Mark 1:35; Luke 3:21; 9:28; 10:21; 11:1; 23:46; John 1: 1–18; 3:16; 8:22, 42; 17: 1–26; Galatians 3:22; 1 John 4:4–12

Suggested Additional Sources for Reading

- Amy-Jill Levine, *The Misunderstood Jew: The Church and the Scandal of the Jewish Jesus* (HarperOne, 2007).
- Marcus Borg, *Reading the Bible Again for the First Time* (HarperSanFrancisco, 2001).
- Walter Wink, *Jesus and Nonviolence: A Third Way* (Fortress Press, 2003).
- Eknath Easwaran, *Gandhi the Man: The Story of His Transformation* (Nilgiri Press, 1997).

Suggested Questions for Further Discussion/Thought

1. Which do you believe is more important: faith in Jesus or the faith of Jesus? Why?
2. Christian refers to "those who embrace the spirit of Christ" in his response. Do you think it's possible to go to heaven, even if you don't claim Jesus as Lord and Savior? Why or why not?
3. If God condemns sacrifice as an act of worship thousands of years before Jesus is even born, is it possible that Jesus was crucified for the forgiveness of sin?
4. How do you view Jesus' relationship to God? Are they one and the same?
5. Have you considered whether Jesus saves us in any other way than by dying on the cross?

25. Was Jesus a pacifist?

Jarrod McKenna

Who is...
Jarrod McKenna

I do like walks on the beach (I would mention surfing but it might mislead people to think I'm cooler than I really am).

No.

Jesus did not come to bring peace but a sword. And we as disciples must wield the same sword Jesus brings, and no other. The question is, what is this sword?

What is this sword that heals rather than harms enemies?

What is this sword that never collaborates or mirrors the powers, thereby exposing their addiction to violence?

What is this sword that prophetically turns over tables of idolatry and injustice in a judgment that does not harm, hurt, coerce, or kill anyone?

What is this fire that is ablaze with the very presence of I Am in response to the cries of the oppressed, this fire that does not destroy the bush in which it burns?

What is this power that is ablaze on the cross, sucking the oxygen of injustice and violence from creation, which then causes a cosmic backdraft in the resurrection, setting the world alight with the love that conquers death?

This sword of Christ is something far more dangerous and dynamic than a philosophy of an ideal, static, passive peace read back onto the life of Christ. Martin Luther King Jr. would insist it is a peace that "is not the absence of tension but the presence of justice." It is the mystery our Lord Jesus embodies, enabling a new world where what we once wasted on bombs is now used to feed the hungry.

Jesus is no pacifist. He is YHWH's nonviolent Suffering Servant whose grace calls us to share in his tears over what would make for peace, whose Spirit empowers us to take up the sword of nonviolence as our only weapon in witness to the victory Christ has won.

Chris Haw

Who is...
Chris Haw

I have a 1-year-old son.

A. The Temple cleansing would seem to imply, "no." But we must be careful to note here how he did not kill (or even, it seems, harm) anybody in this well-documented incident. And the early Jesus followers seem to have taken no inspiration from this story as a type of action to imitate, as we have no documentation of *early* Christians carrying swords or rioting after Jesus' famous "Put your sword back into its place; for all who take the sword will perish by the sword" (Matthew 26:52).

In sum, nothing in the canon contradicts Jesus' oft-ignored teaching, "Love your enemies." And seeing as he gives three concrete examples of how to do so in practice, I do not think he meant this metaphorically, or as Luther pontificated—that one can kill one's enemy and love them at the same time.

In an etymologically strict sense, it is probably beneficial to think that Jesus' politics did involve attempts to "pacify" one's enemy. Walking an extra mile with the demanding officer is just one attempt at pacification. Granted, his speaking truth to his accusers ("why did you hit me?") could have perhaps enflamed their hatred—though I am inclined to think of the enflaming as the fault of the violent, not the lamb.

R. M. Keelan Downton

Who is...
R. M. Keelan Downton

I didn't know I was a European citizen until after my twenty-first birthday.

A. It is clear that Jesus is doing something different when he tells his disciples to respond to being slapped, robbed, or forced to work with a creative response that would evoke shame or other complications for the abuser. It is less clear whether Jesus ever intended this to be scaled up to the level of nation-state (which, of course, hadn't been invented, but like empire, requires significant levels of violence to maintain).

Discussions of whether Jesus is a pacifist get muddled by confusion about the meaning of "violence." I once heard a speaker ask, "How can we reject violence as a means of resisting capitalism? I mean, even Jesus used violence against bankers!" This misses a critical distinction.

To be pacifist means to reject the use of deadly force as a legitimate means of resolving disputes—it does not mean allowing injustice to continue without challenge. It does not mean that those who wish to do violence cannot be constrained legally, economically, or even physically.

The space between inaction and murder is precisely where we see Jesus operating in his dealings with the Roman Empire and the Temple entrepreneurs. Even at the end of Revelation (which some people read as a Rambo-esque return) it is important to remember that the "sword" comes from Jesus' mouth and the blood is Jesus' own.

Tripp Fuller

A. It is perfectly clear that Jesus was against violence and war as means of setting things right. He told his disciples to turn the other cheek, not to resist an evildoer, to pray for their enemies, and then forgave his own enemies from the cross.

But does this make him a pacifist? Would he be one today in our historical situation? Most conversations around this topic quickly devolve into attempts to justify some act of violence (protecting an innocent child) or moral war (putting an end to genocide), yet this misses the larger point of Jesus' embodied teaching. The reason Jesus and God's kingdom reject violence is not because it can't bring about a victory, but because an act of violence leads to a victor who is also a violator of their victims.

Eventually power shifts and the previous victims feel justified in becoming the new violent victors. God's kingdom's way, embodied by Jesus and taught to the disciples, is a way that does not reach victory by building crosses but by bearing them. The ultimate victory of God is a victory for all because through the resurrection, God becomes *victor* by becoming the *victim*.

In doing so God identifies and shares in the suffering of the world and charts a path for reconciliation, even for the violators. This larger perspective reframes the nature of Jesus' "pacifism," asking his followers today not to become passively peaceful but active peacemakers and ambassadors of God's reconciliation.

Scriptural References

Matthew 5:38–48; 2 Corinthians 5:16–21

Suggested Additional Sources for Reading

- John Yoder, *The Politics of Jesus: Vicit Agnus Noster* (Eerdmans, 1972).
- John Yoder, "Peace Without Eschatology; or, If Christ is Truly Lord" in *The Original Revolution: Essays on Christian Pacifism* (Herald Press, 1972).
- André Trocmé, *Jesus and the Nonviolent Revolution* (Herald Press, 1973).
- Walter Wink, *Jesus and Nonviolence: A Third Way* (Fortress Press, 2003).

Suggested Questions for Further Discussion/Thought

1. Do you think the story of Jesus and the money changers in the temple is an example of him being violent? Why or why not?
2. Is there ever a time when violence is justified?
3. Is the violent act of Jesus' crucifixion justifiable? Why or why not?

26. Why would Jesus supply wine for a party as his first "miracle"? Doesn't this seem more like a trick than a miracle? And does this mean he condoned drinking?

Mark Van Steenwyk

Who is...
Mark Van Steenwyk

I met my wife at a Bible camp when we were fourteen years old.

So Jesus goes to a wedding party. Partway through the festivities (which could last for up to seven days), the wine runs out. So Jesus, after being talked into it by his mother, decides to turn about 120 to 180 gallons of water into high-quality wine. Not much of a first miracle, is it? Especially considering his second miracle was healing an official's dying son.

But I think the miracle works on two levels. First, on the practical level, it shows that Jesus isn't unconcerned with everyday sorts of troubles. In other words, if Jesus could help a young couple out of a socially awkward situation after some gentle prodding from his mother then there is hope that Jesus doesn't reserve his compassion for the huge issues of our lives.

But there is something deeper going on, I think. Jesus never wastes a miracle. His miracles always communicate something of God's deep passion for us.

When Jesus turned water into wine, he transformed it into *good* wine. Anyone who is really into wine will tell you about the complexity and difficulty in making a good bottle of wine. And since Cana was a small village, Jesus could have gotten away with making twenty gallons of wine (a little wine does, after all, go a long way). So when presented with a modest need for wine, Jesus decides to create a lavish amount of quality wine.

The message here—and it is one continued throughout the gospel of John—is that God is lavish in his affections for us. The new thing he was doing through Jesus was transforming the way things were into something entirely new. The old life was like water, but the new life—the kingdom of God—is like really good wine.

And yes, since Jesus was willing to make a good vintage for folks who had already been drinking all day, we can assume that he condones drinking for most people.

Why would Jesus supply wine for a party as his first "miracle"?

Christian Piatt

A. There's really nowhere in the Bible that tells us not to drink. On the contrary, Jesus served wine at the passover meal with his disciples, which was to be his last before death. There are warnings, though, about drunkenness.

As for the miracle itself, I've heard it argued that Jesus, being just a boy, was still in his less mature people-pleasing mode. What preteen, after all, wouldn't want to be the hit of the party by providing the masses with all the wine they could drink?

More likely, the story is a metaphor for the promise of God's kingdom, in which there will always be enough and no one will thirst or hunger. Is this kingdom image only something to come after death? Maybe, but some might also suggest that the only way to peace, as illuminated by Jesus, is to invoke the kingdom here and now by liberating ourselves from our tyrannical enslavement to want itself and to release our grip on the material world to share with all who thirst.

Finally, some comment on the high quality of the wine. It's pointed out that most hosts would serve a little bit of the good stuff early on, and then switch to cheaper vintages once peoples' palettes were dulled. However, Jesus offers the best wine last. This could be taken many ways, as can most stories about Jesus, but I like to think it's his way of saying, "You think this is good stuff? You ain't seen nothin' yet!"

Becky Garrison

Who is...
Becky Garrison

My first writing was a one-act play that was an anti-Nixon rant.

A. The real miracle wasn't that Jesus changed water into wine but that Jesus' responded to his mother's request to keep the party happening. Thus marks a hallmark of Jesus' ministry—love triumphs legalism. So sorry to all you Baptist believers, but while Jesus was no drunkard, he did *not* turn water into Welch's grape juice. Nor did he serve saltines at the Last Supper, but I digress.

Scriptural References

John 2:1–11

Why would Jesus supply wine for a party as his first "miracle"?

Suggested Additional Sources for Reading

- Graham Twelftree, *Jesus the Miracle Worker: A Historical and Theological Study* (IVP Academic, 1999).
- N. T. Wright, *Jesus and the Victory of God* (Augsburg Fortress Press, 1997).

Suggested Questions for Further Discussion/Thought

1. What does it mean that Jesus' first recorded miracle took place in the context of a feast?
2. What does this story about Jesus suggest to you about our own approach to self-discipline? Is there ever room in Christianity for consumption of things we want but don't need?
3. Some Christians argue for abstinence from alcohol by suggesting the "wine" in scripture was not actually fermented. Why do you think this is? Does it matter to you?

27. Where was Jesus for the time between his death and resurrection?

José F. Morales Jr.

Who is...
José F. Morales Jr.

I love sweet tea.

"He descended into hell." (The Apostles Creed—second century C.E.)

"Sheol saw me and was shattered, and Death ejected me and many with me . . . And I made a congregation of living among his dead." (*Odes of Solomon* 42:11, 14—second century C.E.)

"When he ascended on high, he made captivity itself a captive . . . When it says, 'He ascended,' what does it mean but that he had also descended into the lower parts of the earth." (Ephesians 4:8–9)

A. As demonstrated in these early Christian writings, the early Church believed that Jesus went to hell—historically called "the descent into hell"—to rescue the righteous awaiting vindication (also see, Matthew 27:50–53; 1 Peter 3:18–19). By "hell," they meant the Hebrew notion of Sheol—a waiting place not as horrific as Dante's *Inferno*, but not exactly a vacation either. Jesus went "down there" not because he "deserved" it but because according to Jewish belief at the time, *all* went to Sheol to await judgment, and for the righteous, bodily resurrection.

The early Christians (mostly Jews who accepted Jesus as the *resurrected* Messiah) deviated from the rest of their Jewish (Pharisaic) comrades, in that they believed that bodily resurrection, which was to occur at the *end* of history, was initiated *in* history through Christ. "But in fact Christ has been raised from the dead, the first fruits of those who have died" (1 Corinthians 15:20).

Jesus, "the first fruits of the resurrection," enters into death's home. But death could not contain him; nor could death contain those he claims. Ode 42 of the *Odes of Solomon* proclaims, "Sheol saw me and was shattered."

This Sheol-shattered moment has been depicted in icons in Old Cairo's Abu Serga Church and in the Chora Monastery outside Istanbul. Both depict Christ crushing hell's gates and following him are Adam and Eve, David, John the Baptist, Abel, and others.

The Orthodox and Coptic Churches have it right in reminding us that resurrection is a communal event.

Before you think I'm asking you to believe in the fantastical, the early church taught this event not as history but as theology. So as Marcus Borg likes to say about all myths, it's not *literally* true, but it's *really* true. Amen![13]

Tripp Fuller

The most ancient creed we have from the early church, the Apostles' Creed, includes the line "he descended into hell" as the plain answer to the question. A number of passages in the Bible hint at such a conclusion, most strongly 1 Peter 3:18–20: "For Christ also suffered for sins once for all, the righteous for the unrighteous, in order to bring you to God. He was put to death in the flesh, but made alive in the spirit, in which also he went and made a proclamation to the spirits in prison, who in former times did not obey."

It's easy to think that this is a crazy idea. We no longer believe the world to be three layers—heaven, earth, and hell—which seems a given in the doctrine. Is hell really in the middle of the earth? But I think we need not too hastily get rid of the idea because it is communicating much more than "where" Jesus was but the magnitude of God's work in Christ.

Before there were any geological concerns the church debated the relevance of the doctrine and decided to keep it for theological reasons. The death and resurrection of Jesus was not something that happened to him but something God did for all, the dead, living, and yet to be born.

The Eastern Orthodox Church believes Jesus not only descended into hell but also conquered it! Charles Wesley penned a hymn in which he proclaims, "Hell, Earth, and Sin with ease overcome! Thy nature and thy name is love!" I don't think we have to believe Jesus somehow ended up in a certain place, more important is that his own death was defeated in the resurrection. That reality is not about location, but rather the power of God's love to reach beyond all limitations—sin and death!

13. Marcus J. Borg and John Dominic Crossan, *The Last Week: A Day-by-Day Account of Jesus's Final Week in Jerusalem* (San Francisco: HarperOne, 2006), 165–87.

R. M. Keelan Downton

Who is...

R. M. Keelan Downton

I have two cats that play fetch like puppies.

A. The traditional answer to this question is included in the creed and repeated by many Christians on a weekly basis: He descended into hell. Whether you think about hell as a place or a state of being or something else entirely, I think this phrase is best understood as "God went where God was not."

Like doing math with infinity, once you grant the resurrection you're thinking about something for which your experience of the world ceases to be relevant—what some Christian traditions mean by "mystery." If you think about the postresurrection experiences described by the disciples in terms of quantum physics (something about phase transitions and multidimensional space-time), the "where" and "time" are part of the same mystery.

For the earliest hearers, the "place" that Jesus went to is far less important than the duration of death—long enough to rule out the first century equivalent of a near-death experience. It is not that Jesus could not die but that Jesus really died and did not stay dead. Even at the end of possibilities that we call death, even in the impossible place where God is not, God becomes present and opens up new possibilities of resurrected life.

Scriptural References

Matthew 27:50–53; 1 Corinthians 15; Ephesians 4:7–10; 1 Peter 3:18–22; 4:6; *Odes of Solomon* 42—this is an early Christian hymnal from the second century C.E. It doesn't not have scriptural status in any Christian communion but . . . what the hell (pun intended)!

Suggested Additional Sources for Reading

- Marcus J. Borg and John Dominic Crossan, "Saturday," in *The Last Week: The Day-by-Day Account of Jesus's Final Week in Jerusalem* (HarperOne, 2006).
- Jerry Walls et al., "What to Say about Hell—A Symposium," *Christian Century*, June 3, 2008, http://www.christiancentury.org/article.lasso?id=4809.
- Garry Wills, "Descent into Hell," in *What Jesus Meant* (Penguin, 2007).

Suggested Questions for Further Discussion/Thought

1. Does this early Christian tradition of Jesus' "descent into hell" excite you or trouble you? Why?
2. What role, if any, should this and other early Christian traditions play in Christian formation and discipleship?
3. Read 1 Corinthian 15. What do you think about bodily resurrection? About eternal life?
4. Discuss hell. Is it a place or state of being? Do you believe it exists? If so, for what purpose? Do you have to die to be in hell?

Question

28. Most of our images of Jesus portray him with long blond or brown hair, blue eyes, and white skin. But what did Jesus really look like?

Jarrod McKenna

Our Peace Tree Community's main houses are in a neighborhood with a high aboriginal population, which is an amazing blessing. We practice hospitality to people in need and we had one young woman staying with us who was struggling to get off hard drugs and several times disappeared, leaving her children with us for days. One evening, driving her back from an appointment, she said something that would make any Christian's heart sing: "I want to become a Christian. I'm not going to see my kids grow up if I don't."

My eyes teared up with gratitude for answered prayers for her deliverance from cycles of destruction. Yet her next sentence turned my praise to lament: "God's got to stop me acting black."

That sentence haunts me. The colonization of her imagination was so total that she had identified her skin color with sin and God with the white, Western society. Prayerfully I responded, "Jesus won't stop you acting black. He'll teach you to act black. He'll teach you the dignity of being a beautiful child of God. Don't believe the paintings in churches and the movies that show Jesus as a wajella [white fella]. When Jesus was on [E]arth, he looked more like you than me. He was a Middle Eastern man with people from North Africa in his family tree. His people were oppressed and their land taken from them, just like yours. Yet, he came and broke all the powers of death by dying for us all, even his oppressors. Then God raised him victorious over all that would keep us from knowing the beauty and dignity we have in him."

Later I shared that story with "Pop Allan," an aboriginal elder in my area. He said to me, "Until my people realize we are to be in the image of Christ, not the image of the colonizers, we won't be free." Amen.

Lord, free us all from the image of colonizers so we might be conformed to the image of your Son.

Becky Garrison

When I toured around Nazareth, I didn't see any natives that resembled this white wimpy Jesus that's depicted in the vast majority of western European and North American churches. Rather these residents possessed a dark olive complexion replete with dark hair and full beards, in the case of men. Hence the Messiah looked Mediterranean.

José F. Morales Jr.

Who is...
José F. Morales Jr.

I think graffiti is a legitimate art and should be treated as such.

A. I can't remember where I heard this profound truth: "God made us in God's image, and so we decided to return the favor." This is true about our images of Jesus.

For the last several decades, a movement within New Testament scholarship called "the Jesus Seminar" has tried to unearth the "historical Jesus"— that is, the Jesus behind the modern cultural depictions, behind the classic creeds of the faith, and even behind the gospels themselves. Their project is based on the assumption that the gospels contain both the actual words of Jesus and the words that the earliest Christians put in his mouth.

Now some of the work toward the "historical Jesus" has shed new light on Jesus of Nazareth and the faith he inspired, including a reclaiming of Jesus' cultural-religious identity as a Palestinian Jewish peasant, which means he probably didn't look Scandinavian.

Still, Scot McKnight notes, even the folks at the Jesus Seminar are just as susceptible as the premodern church before them, of making a Jesus in their image and likeness who resembles their biases and values: Jesus as a self-promoting academic (though he lived in a mainly preliterate, communal culture) who didn't perform miracles (because academia deems miracles "irrational").[14]

The common question in the United States has been, Was Jesus "black" or "white"? First of all, as someone who is "brown" (Latino), I feel left out. Second, the philosopher Cornel West reminds us that those racial terms are modern constructs from a racialized world obsessed with power. Paul didn't use those terms to talk about Jesus. Jesus was a Galilean, a Palestinian Jew with (more than likely) bronze skin due to genetics and sunburn. So as West jokingly noted, he probably looked more like Isaac Hayes than Jim Caviezel.[15]

This reminds me of a joke: A black man and a white man, on their way up to heaven, argue if Jesus is white or black. When they get to the pearly gates, they ask Peter. Peter says, "Ask him yourself. Hey, Jesus! These guys want to know if you're black or white." And Jesus responds, "¿Que?"

---

14. Scot McKnight, "The Jesus We'll Never Know," *Christianity Today* 54, no. 4 (April 2010): 22–26.

15. Cornel West, "Democracy Matter" (lecture, University of Chicago, March 2, 2006).

Scriptural References

Genesis 1:26–27; Deuteronomy 26:5–9; Proverbs 14:31; Psalm 10:14; Isaiah 25:4; 41:17; Matthew 13:54–58; 25:31–46; Luke 4:16–21; 2 Corinthians 8:9; Colossians 1:15; Hebrews 1:3a; Revelation 1:12–16

Suggested Additional Sources for Reading

- Scott Korb, *Life in Year One: What the World Was Like in First-Century Palestine* (Riverhead, 2010).
- Rainbow Spirit Elders, *Rainbow Spirit Theology* (ATF Press, 2008).
- Dave Andrews, *Christi-Anarchy* (Lion, 2001).
- S. Wesley Ariarajah, *Gospel and Culture: An Ongoing Discussion within the Ecumenical Movement*, pamphlet 1, *Gospel and Cultures* (WCC, 1995).
- James Cone, *Black Theology and Black Power* (Seabury Press, 1969).
- Vine Deloria Jr., *God Is Red: A Native View of Religion* (Grosset & Dunlap, 1973).
- Virgilio Elizondo, *Galilean Journey: The Mexican American Promise* (Orbis, 1983).
- Jacqueline Grant, *White Women's Christ and Black Women's Jesus: Feminist Christology and Womanist Response* (Scholars Press, 1989).
- Neil MacGregor and Erika Langmuir, *Seeing Salvation: Images of Christ in Art* (Yale Univ. Press, 2000).
- Scot McKnight, "The Jesus We'll Never Know," *Christianity Today*, April 2010, 22–26.
- Jaroslav Pelikan, *Jesus through the Centuries: His Place in the History of Culture* (Yale Univ. Press, 1985).
- Elisabeth Schüssler Fiorenza, *Jesus and the Politics of Interpretation* (Continuum, 2000).
- Geza Vermes, *The Changing Faces of Jesus* (Viking Compass, 2001).

Suggested Questions for Further Discussion/Thought

1. Why do people tend to depict Jesus in their own image?
2. Jarrod talked about "Pop Allan's" take on the story. What's yours? Do you preach a Jesus with whom oppressed people can identify?
3. When you close your eyes and imagine Jesus, what does he look like? What factors do you think influence your image of Jesus?
4. Do you see any issues with Jesus being male? Why or why not?
5. Jesus was Jewish, not a Christian. How does this historical truth impact the Christian faith?

29. Who do people of the Jewish faith believe Jesus was? A prophet? Just a man? Why don't they believe he was the Messiah?

José F. Morales Jr.

Who is...
José F. Morales Jr.

I'm a morning person and a night owl, which means that around 3 p.m. I'm completely useless.

The Jews' concerns with Jesus stem from three issues: Christian behavior toward Jews, the oneness of God, and the gospel accounts of Jesus as God and Messiah.

Christian Anti-Semitism

Over the centuries, Christians have misunderstood Jesus and Paul and have used their anti-Semitic interpretations against Jews and their faith. The Spanish Inquisition was done *in the name of Christ*, though Jesus was Jewish and so was Paul, who made it clear, "I ask, then, has God rejected his people? By no means! I myself am an Israelite" (Romans 11.1).

"God is One"

To claim Jesus as God or divine violates the *Shema*, which is a cornerstone text in Judaism: "Hear, O Israel: The LORD is our God, the LORD alone" (Deuteronomy 6:4). Of course, for Christians, monotheism is also nonnegotiable, hence, the Trinity. The doctrine of the Trinity is seen as heretical to Jews (and Muslims).

Jesus of the Gospels vs. the Jesus of History

Lastly, recent scholarship asserts that the Gospels are a combination of historical memory of and theological interpretation about Jesus—in other words, what the actual human Jesus really said, and what his early followers said about him. The later theological layering of Jesus (e.g., Jesus' messianic claims, Jesus as the "Word" of God) violates Jewish understanding of divine oneness and goes against Jewish messianic expectation. For many Jews, the Messiah will liberate the Holy Land, and lead the Jewish Diaspora (and Gentile believers) back to that land (Isaiah 60; 2 Chronicles 36:22–23). Jesus did neither; hence he is not the Messiah.

Jesus has been questionable to Jews, and rightly so. Now in recent work on the historical Jesus, some Jews have been willing to claim him as their own. Geza Vermes, a Jewish scholar of Jesus, concludes that the human Jesus (before Christians "Christianized" him) was a rabbi and a revival preacher of Israel (Matthew 10:5–7). About *this* Jesus, Vermes says, "As for the open-minded and unprejudiced Jews, [Jesus] . . . must appear to them as familiar, friendly, attractive and profoundly impressive figure who has something significant and unifying to offer, which Jews can share with mankind [*sic*] at large."[16]

Interestingly, Islam shares more in common with Christians when it comes to Jesus. Though he is neither God, nor God's Son, nor a "person of the Trinity," the Muslim Jesus is a prophet "of the highest order," the bringer of the good news and the kingdom of God, *al masih* (the messiah), "God's Word cast to Mary," and the one who will judge humanity at the end of the age.[17]

Peter J. Walker

Who is...
Peter J. Walker

I listen to hardcore gangster rap but secretly want to perform in a boy band.

When I first read this question, I confess I started to answer it. Then it occurred to me: I have never had a Jewish person tell me what she or he believed about Jesus. What I have heard comes mostly from Christian word of mouth. It goes something like this: The Jews are God's chosen people, but they have rejected Jesus. They are still waiting for a messiah, which is why Christians are now the spiritual recipients of God's promises to Abraham. Sounds sort of arrogant, doesn't it? I'm sure that's not the story Jewish people tell about themselves.

I live in the Pacific Northwest, which is not the most cosmopolitan region of the United States. I don't know any practicing Jews. I met some folks who called themselves "Jews for Jesus" once, but they weren't actually Jewish; they were former evangelicals.

16. Geza Vermes, *The Authentic Gospel of Jesus* (New York: Penguin, 2003), 417.

17. Seyyed Hossein Nasr, "We and You: Let Us Meet in God's Love" (lecture, *"Love of God, Love of Neighbour,"* The First Muslim-Catholic Forum Conference, Vatican City, 4–6 November 2008), http://www.acommonword.com; "A Muslim Message of Thanks and of Christmas Greetings" (open letter to all Christians from Muslim leaders and scholars throughout the world, December 23, 2007), http://www.acommonword.com.

I'm reminded of an ad that aired on a major Christian radio network shortly after the September 11th terrorist attacks in 2001. It clearly differentiated between Allah and the God of Christianity. The reasoning seemed to be that the more Christianity distanced itself from Islam, the safer it would be from repercussions against radical religion. But it was an example of Christians reducing another faith down to simplified bullet points, organized to make an argument. Christian radio was speaking for 1.5 billion Muslims, and it wasn't very flattering.

Christians don't like being mischaracterized. It's important we are equally committed to not mischaracterizing the faith of our neighbors. That involves initiating real relationships with people from other backgrounds. Friendship changes everything, and if we're passionate about learning, rather than obsessed with conversion, beautiful things can happen. And our questions get answered.

Lee C. Camp

Who is...
Lee C. Camp

I still enjoy writing custom software, and my undergraduate degree was in computer science.

It depends on the Jew! We should not overlook that Jesus was a Jew, as well as every single one of the early believers. To become a believer in Jesus as Messiah did not mean that Jews were no longer Jews. Many continued the various practices of the old covenant, such as the festivals and circumcision.

But many Jews then and many Jews now do not believe Jesus to have been the anticipated Messiah. Some of the early pagan and early Jewish critics of the early church said that Jesus could not have *possibly* been the expected Messiah, because the prophets claimed that when the Messiah comes, war will be undone, and the nations will learn war no more. The nations still wage war: Thus Jesus could not have been the Messiah.

There was a fascinating response among many of the early church fathers to this very legitimate objection: The church, they responded in effect, comprises people from every tongue and every tribe, and we who once waged war against our enemies wage war no more (all the early church fathers, until the time of the early fourth century, taught that Christians are called by Jesus not to wage war). In other words, the very existence of the peaceable church was the most viable apologetic, or defense, of the claim that Jesus was indeed the Messiah.

And so our question may get turned back on us: How can Jews or pagans who do not believe Jesus to be the Messiah believe otherwise if the church is not a faithful embodiment of the way of Christ? Given that members of the modern church in one nation often wage war against members of the church in other nations, how can we overcome the early Jews' objections to the Messiahship of Jesus?

Scriptural References

Deuteronomy 6:4–9; 2 Chronicles 36:22–23; Isaiah 2; 9; 60; Micah 4; Matthew 10:5–10

Suggested Additional Sources for Reading

- Marcus Borg, *Jesus and Buddha: The Parallel Sayings* (Ulysses Press, 1997).
- A Common Word between Us and You: http://www.acommonword .com.
- Tarif Khalidi, ed. and trans., *The Muslim Jesus: Sayings and Stories in Islamic Literature* (Harvard Univ. Press, 2001).
- Seyyed Hossein Nasr, "We and You—Let Us Meet in God's Love" (paper, "Love of God, Love of Neighbor": First Catholic-Muslim Forum Conference, Vatican City, November 4–6, 2008), http://www .acommonword.com.
- Geza Vermes, *The Authentic Gospel of Jesus* (Allen Lane, 2003).
- Geza Vermes, *The Changing Faces of Jesus* (Viking Compass, 2001).
- Amy-Jill Levine, *The Misunderstood Jew: The Church and the Scandal of the Jewish Jesus* (HarperOne, 2007).
- "Why Don't Jews Believe In Jesus?," http://www.simpletoremember .com/articles/a/jewsandjesus.
- Messiah Truth Project: http://www.messiahtruth.com.
- Jews for Jesus: http://www.jewsforjesus.org.

Suggested Questions for Further Discussion/Thought

1. In what ways might the life of your own church support or undercut the claim that "Jesus is the Messiah"?
2. If a person from another faith asked you to tell them about Jesus, what would you say?
3. What do you make of the striking similarities between the Christian and Muslim beliefs about Jesus?
4. Read about a Jewish perspective on Jesus at http://www.simpletoremember .com/articles/a/jewsandjesus, watch the video, and discuss whether a Jewish understanding of God is easier to believe in than a Christian understanding.
5. How do you feel about these Jewish arguments against traditional Christian interpretations of Messiahship in the Hebrew Bible (Old Testament)?
6. Explore what it might feel like for a Jewish person hearing Christian testimony about Jesus. What might your response(s) be?

30. When Jesus was resurrected, why did he still have wounds on his body?

David Lose

Who is...
David Lose

I was born on the darkest day of the year.

A. All of the gospels are clear that the risen Jesus is also the human Jesus who wept and laughed, taught and fed. He is not a ghost or spirit (Luke 24:37–40), and the reports of his resurrection were not a delusion (John 20:24–29). In short, Jesus has been raised from the dead, and the risen Jesus is the same Jesus the disciples had known and loved. Why does this matter? Two reasons.

First, resurrection is a promise made to the whole of who we are. Some years ago, I met a woman who preferred the idea of the immortal soul to bodily resurrection. Her husband had died some years earlier, and she found it more comforting to think that his soul had survived death. I asked her whether in the next life she hoped to encounter the "essence" of her dead husband or the real him, warts, scars, and all. Suddenly, "essence" didn't seem quite enough. She realized she longed for *him*—all of him: transformed, to be sure, but not just a spirit. That is what the bodily resurrection promises; God wants more than our essence for eternity. God wants—and will have—all of us.

Second, resurrection promises that God understands who and what we are. In the incarnation we see God in Jesus passionately embrace all that it is to be human—our hopes, dreams, possibilities, and limitations. In the cross, we see God remain faithful to that human condition—faithful to us—to the very end. In the resurrection, we see God remain faithful to us *through* the end and into new life. The resurrection does not leave incarnation and crucifixion behind but transforms them.

Similarly, the scar-bearing, risen Jesus does not leave us behind but promises us transformation as well.

Jarrod McKenna

A. It's interesting that the disciples don't notice the wounds on the stranger that walks with them on the road to Emmaus. Nor on the hungry visitor that is present at their table. It seems that the disciples only recognize that Jesus still had wounds on his body when he is engaging them in their doubt (Luke 24:39; John 20:24–28). Thomas does scandalously proclaim, "My Lord and my God" but only after Jesus meets him in his doubt by revealing his wounds.

A Lord who reigns with wounds? A victim who is victoriously free from retaliation? A God who meets us in our doubt and simply asks that we reach out our hand and touch the kingdom in wounds that heal?

When I worked, caring for people with disabilities, I started reading to a man who dedicated his whole life to doing just that in a L'Arche community. Henri Nouwen wrote,

> Nobody escapes being wounded. We all are wounded people, whether physically, emotionally, mentally, or spiritually. The main question is not 'How can we hide our wounds?' so we don't have to be embarrassed, but 'How can we put our woundedness in the service of others?' When our wounds cease to be a source of shame, and become a source of healing, we have become wounded healers.
>
> Jesus is God's wounded healer: through his wounds we are healed. Jesus' suffering and death brought joy and life. His humiliation brought glory; his rejection brought a community of love. As followers of Jesus we can also allow our wounds to bring healing to others.[18]

Cornel West, drawing on Nouwen, urges us to become "wounded healers, not wounded hurters." God transforms the very things we long to be freed from into a source of freedom that witnesses to the resurrection. Thanks be to God.

Tripp Fuller

Who is...
Tripp Fuller

When I retire I want to front a Rolling Stones cover band.

The most obvious answer is that the body that was raised is the one that was crucified. Yet this assertion, though it may be true, can misdirect the Christian from the profundity that the risen Christ retained his wounds. Many New Testament scholars would argue that the wounds of Jesus recorded in the gospels were narrated rebuttals to a heresy called docetism, which rejected the humanity of Jesus because the fullness of

---

18. Henri J. M. Nouwen, *The Wounded Healer: Ministry in Contemporary Society* (New York: Image, 1979).

humanity was less than appropriate and compatible with what it means to be God. They argued that Jesus only appeared to be human.

If the resurrected Christ had wounds then you have an embodied Jesus who died a real death and conquered it as the Crucified One. It is as if from the very birth of the church it was inappropriate to think of the resurrected Jesus without also remembering the cross-dead Christ. This remains a challenge to us today.

For example, it is easy to get so distracted by the hope we have in the risen Christ that our focus turns from this world toward God's future, but here, it is essential to remember that the risen Christ who "ascended to the right hand of the Father" is a wounded Son. At God's right hand is the Son whose wounds testify to the brokenness of our violent world and call us to be a part of God, transforming what is into something new. That is precisely why a real crucified and wounded body being raised was and is important to the Christian imagination.

José F. Morales Jr.

The resurrection tradition in the story of Jesus is a myth. I don't mean "myth" the way we commonly use it—that is, a lie—but the way it's used in anthropology: A "myth" is a story that makes sense of reality at its deepest level. Myths may or may not be historically or factually true, but they are *really* true, *profoundly* true. (With this said, I do believe that the empty tomb was a historical event.)

When John writes in chapter 20 of the encounter between doubting Thomas and the resurrected-yet-wounded Christ, he was trying to teach us about the deeper meaning of life and Jesus' role in that.

In his conception in Mary, Jesus redeemed all wombs. In his birth, Jesus redeemed all life. At his death, he redeemed all tombs. In short, there's nowhere we can go where God in Christ hasn't been.

Within this larger "mythical" framework, we can gain an appreciation for the wounds of Jesus. Through his wounds, our wounds are redeemed. Woundedness does not have the last word. Rather, out of death comes life; and out of woundedness, healing. It's through the wounds of Jesus that Thomas is healed of his own woundedness—his wounds of pain and doubt.

This, in my opinion, is one of the most powerful and pastoral texts in scripture. For in it, we are assured that even our wounds can be used for resurrecting purposes and that out of our woundedness comes healing, restoration, and wholeness for others.

As Henri Nouwen proclaims, we are "wounded healers" who have the power to heal others in the name of Jesus the wounded one. This gives new meaning to Isaiah's prophecy "by his bruises we are healed" (Isaiah 53:5).

Scriptural References

Isaiah 53; Luke 24:39; John 20:19–31

Suggested Additional Sources for Reading

- David Lose, *Making Sense of the Christian Faith* (Augsburg Fortress Press, 2010).
- Henri Nouwen, *The Wounded Healer: Ministry in Contemporary Society* (Doubleday, 1972).
- Nancy L. Eiesland, *The Disabled God: Toward a Liberatory Theology of Disability* (Abingdon Press, 1994).
- Mark Lewis Taylor, *The Executed God: The Way of the Cross in Lockdown America* (Fortress Press, 2001).

Suggested Questions for Further Discussion/Thought

1. Share moments when your wounds were of healing and inspiration to others and when others shared their wounds to inspire and heal you.
2. In light of this take on redeemed woundedness, how should we read Isaiah 53?
3. What are wounds in your life that you still haven't healed from?
4. How can we avoid having our wounds becoming our identity and instead find our identity in Christ so our wounds can "become a source of healing"?

31. Does Jesus ever refer to the Trinity (Father, Son, and Holy Spirit) in his ministry? If so, does he identify himself as part of that Trinity? If not, where did it come from?

Jarrod McKenna

Some think "the Trinity" is Greek (i.e., "pagan") thinking, perverting Jewish "monotheism." For me the beauty and radical teaching of the Triune God is not a delusion but a spectacular affirmation of Jewish monotheism transformed in light of the nonviolent Christ.

The central prayer of Jewish resistance to pagan empires, the *Shema* (literally in Hebrew: *hear*), "Hear, O Israel: The LᴄʀᴅA is our God, the LᴄʀᴅA alone" (Deuteronomy 6:4) was a defense against the "gods" of empire. In the earliest writing of the Christians, the *Shema* is affirmed yet transfigured in light of the resurrection. As seen in 1 Corinthians 8:6, the crucified nonviolent Messiah Jesus is inescapably placed into the center of the *Shema*: "[F]or us there is one God, the Father, from whom are all things and for whom we exist, and one Lord, Jesus Christ, through whom are all things and through whom we exist" (1 Corinthians 8:6).

Not just in John's gospel but throughout the synoptics we are asked to *Shema* (hear!) that Jesus of Nazareth, the Father, and the Holy Spirit are seen in dynamic relationship as "the Lord our God [who] is one" (just read the baptism of Jesus in Mark 1:9–11). The one true Creator God who is fully revealed in Jesus to be nonviolently liberating all creation from all domination, violence, and oppression.

As Saint Gregory of Nyssa put it, "All that the Father is, we see revealed in the Son . . . who through the Spirit works all things . . . We envisage a strange and paradoxical diversity in unity and unity in diversity."[19]

Jesus doesn't refer to the Trinity; he reveals the Trinity. And he makes a way for us to participate in the love of the triune God that he reveals nonviolently redeeming all of creation. Let all of creation *Shema*.

Brandon Gilvin

The Trinity is not, strictly speaking, a biblical concept. However, the three "persons" of the Trinity are mentioned throughout the New Testament. The God of Israel is obviously a central figure throughout both the Hebrew Scriptures and the New Testament. The entire New Testament hinges on the ministry of Jesus.

---

19. K. Ware, *The Orthodox Way* (New York: St. Vladimir's Seminary Press), 31.

The Spirit plays a trickier role. It has often been noted that the book of Genesis uses the term *Spirit of God* in its opening lines (Genesis 1:2). Many commentators find parallels between the Spirit and "Lady Wisdom" in the Book of Proverbs. The church is transformed and invigorated at Pentecost from Luke to Acts and in John, Jesus refers to a paraclete, translated as "comforter" or "advocate," who will follow him.

It wasn't until the following centuries that theologians attempted to systematize these traditions and explain how God could be one, be present as a "Spirit," and be incarnate as Jesus.

Tertullian, a third century C.E. theologian, was likely the first person to use the term *trinity* to describe the relationship between the three. While the word trinity may not appear anywhere in the Bible, its components can be found there.

Pablo A. Jiménez

Who is...
Pablo A. Jiménez

I am the father of three children: Antonio, Paola, and Natalia.

A. The early church developed the term *trinity* as a theological concept after the gospels were already written. Therefore, no one—not even Jesus—refers to the Divine as "the Trinity" in the Bible.

The closest that the Bible comes to affirm the doctrine of the Trinity is 1 John 5:7, which reads, "There are three that testify," referring to the Spirit, the water, and the blood mentioned in verse 8. However, older translations of the Bible include a phrase now largely seen as an "interpolation" or addition in verse 7: "There are three that testify in heaven, the Father, the Word and the Holy Spirit, and these are one." Recent translations of the Bible relegate this interpolation to a footnote.

Nonetheless, this does not mean that the Trinity is not biblical or that its basic premise is mistaken. The Trinity is a concept developed by the church in order to affirm that there is only one God, at the same time that it affirmed the divinity of Jesus and the Holy Spirit.

The gospels clearly affirm that there is only one God. However, they also affirm that Jesus was the "Son of God," sharing his divine nature. And the Holy Spirit is the Spirit of God and the Spirit of Christ. The risen Christ is present today through the Holy Spirit. Therefore, the gospels, in particular, and the New Testament, in general, affirm a paradox: There is only one God, although Jesus and the Holy Spirit are also divine. The Trinity offers a theological explanation of this paradox.

Scriptural References

Proverbs 1–9; Matthew 28:19; John 14:16, 26; 15:26; 16:7; Acts 2; 1 Corinthians 8:1–6; 2 Corinthians 13:14; Galatians 4:1–7; Philippians 2:5–11; Colossians 1:15–20; 1 John 5:7–8

Suggested Additional Sources for Reading

- N. T. Wright, *The Challenge of Jesus* (InterVarsity Press, 1999).
- J. H. Yoder, *The War of the Lamb: The Ethics of Nonviolence and Peacemaking* (Brazos Press, 2009).
- K. Ware, *The Orthodox Way* (St. Vladimir's Seminary Press, 1995).
- J. N. D. Kelly, *Early Christian Doctrines* (A. & C. Black, 1958).
- Henry Chadwick, *The Early Church* (Hodder & Stoughton, 1968).
- Justo Gonzalez, *The Story of Christianity*, vol. 1 (HarperOne, 2010).
- Karen Armstrong, *A History of God* (Ballantine, 1994).
- J. W. McClendon Jr., *Systematic Theology*, vol. 2, *Doctrine* (Abingdon Press, 1994).
- N. T. Wright, *The New Testament and the People of God* (Fortress Press, 1992).
- N. T. Wright, *What St. Paul Really Said* (Eerdmans, 1997).

Suggested Questions for Further Discussion/Thought

1. How do the ways you imagine God connect with your understanding of the Trinity? How do they differ?
2. How do you see the expressions of God within the Trinity as connected, as well as distinct?
3. How might the doctrine of the Triune God be a form of resistance to those empires and powers that want an ethic found in "God" that contradicts what's revealed in Jesus?
4. Kallistos Ware says, "The Trinity is not a philosophical theory but the living God whom we worship; and so there comes a point in our approach to the Trinity when argumentation and analysis must give place to wordless prayer." Does your understanding of God as Trinity lead you to more words and arguments or more worship and prayer?

Question

32. What are the Jesus papers? Are they true? What do they mean to the Christian faith?

Sherri Emmons

Who is...
Sherri Emmons

I ate cat one time, by accident.

A. Michael Baigent titled his book *The Jesus Papers* after papyrus documents he claimed to see in the possession of an unnamed private collector. He claims the papers are letters written by Jesus to the Jewish court several years after the crucifixion—proof, Baigent says, that the crucifixion was "rigged," that Jesus survived the cross, and that he was spirited away by his friends and his wife, Mary Magdalene.

It's a great conspiracy theory, but Baigent offers not a shred of proof to back up his claims. My biggest problem with the theory is not the lack of evidence, however, or the great conspiracy Baigent claims the Vatican has engaged in to cover up "the truth." It is that Baigent depicts Jesus as a con man, conspiring with the disciples (and Pontius Pilate) to convince the Jewish authorities that he was dead, and then escaping to France. That image just doesn't jive with the Jesus we see in the gospels.

L. Shannon Moore

A. Call me unread, dumb, or blissfully ignorant, but I never heard of *The Jesus Papers* until I got this question sent to me. So like Michael Scott on *The Office* and nearly every college freshman working on that first term paper, I turned to the encyclopedia of the new millennium for help: Wikipedia (go ahead and admit it. You use it too. You probably even use it as a verb—"I Wikipedia'd it").

I found some good information there to get me pointed in the right direction, but figuring the editor would not be satisfied with information gleaned from that source, I branched out to more reliable forms of information—like the *New York Times* and the *Christian Research Journal*.

The Jesus Papers is a book written in 2006 by Michael Baigent. In it, the author spins a *Da Vinci Code*—like tale in which Jesus marries Mary Magdalene, fakes his death on the cross (with the help of the Roman governor, Pontius Pilate), and moves to Egypt (or possibly France) to live out the rest of his life. The problem with this tale is that the author claims it is a true one—based on a letter supposedly written by Jesus himself (a letter that only Baigent and a couple of others have seen).

Critics and scholars alike have largely panned these allegations as preposterous. As for what they mean to the Christian faith, I'll sum it up in a word: nothing.

Suggested Additional Sources for Reading

- Michael Baigent, *The Jesus Papers: Uncovering the Greatest Cover-Up in History* (Harper, 2007).
- Paul L. Maier, "A Summary Critique: The Jesus Papers," *Christian Research Journal* 30, no. 1 (2007), http://journal.equip.org/articles/a-summary-critique-the-jesus-papers.
- Dwight Garner, "This Week in God," *New York Times*, April 16, 2006, http://www.nytimes.com/2006/04/16/books/review/16tbr.html.

Suggested Questions for Further Discussion/Thought

1. Why are people drawn to speculate on scenarios about Jesus that are so wildly different from biblical texts? Is it because of the scripture, religious institutions, and so on?
2. Do you think Christianity would be significantly affected it if were discovered that Jesus had not died on the cross (and consequently was not resurrected)? Could the religion survive?

Question

Pablo A. Jiménez

A. Matthew, Mark, and Luke are very similar. Experts think that Mark was the main source used by Matthew and Luke to write their gospels. These documents are so similar that experts in biblical studies have given them a particular name: the "synoptic" gospels. The word *synoptic* is derived from two Greek words: *syn*, which means "with" and *ophthalmos*, which means "eye." Therefore they can be read together as "with a single eye."

In the synoptic gospels the disturbance at the Temple is one of the main reasons for Jesus' execution. The Temple courtyard was visible from the watchtowers of the Antonia Fortress, from where Roman soldiers monitored activities. According to the synoptic gospels, Jesus was arrested a few days after this event, which surely labeled him as an enemy of the state.

John, written later than the others, follows his own path. For theological reasons, John places the account of the disturbance at the Temple at the very beginning of his story. It serves as an indictment of the Jewish *status quo*.

Sadly, John refers to Jesus' adversaries as "the Jews," which some people mistakenly understand in ethnic terms. In reality, John's term refers to the established Jewish political and religious leadership, particularly those in collusion with the Roman occupation army.

In historical terms, though, the disturbance did occur in Jesus' last week, triggering his persecution, arrest, torture, sentence, and execution.

Christian Piatt

Who is...
Christian Piatt

*The tendon in my left pinky finger is too short,
which makes my finger permanently crooked.*

It's always interesting when stories differ from one gospel to another. For some, this may present a problem to reconcile, particularly if they require the Bible to be perfect not only in *truth* but also in *fact*.

Another perspective actually can tell us a lot about what was going on within the culture at the time the texts were written. Take this story in the gospels, for example. In *The People's New Testament Commentary*, Eugene Boring and Fred Craddock note that the Temple referred to in the stories in Matthew, Mark, and Luke no longer exists by the time John was written, having been destroyed by war.

This, of course, doesn't mean that John's gospel couldn't have the story happening at the same time as the so-called synoptic gospels. But the destruction of the Temple, foretold by Jesus in scripture, serves too as a metaphor for the understanding within Christianity of where God dwells.

In the Jewish tradition, the Temple is a holier place than others, which means that Jesus was, in a sense, protecting "God's house" in the synoptic gospels. But in John, which was written decades later in the life of the early Christian movement, Jesus is establishing himself as the new focus of God's power, carried out into the world by the "body of Christ," that is, his followers.

So the difference comes down to a matter of priorities. In the synoptics, Jesus' appearance at the Temple is one of the final challenges to the powers that be, leading to his death. In John, however, the story is establishing Jesus' divinity, and that he—not the physical church—is now endowed with God's authority.

David Lose

The writers of the four gospels were not writing history as we know it. They were confessing their faith through historical story. Their goal is not neutral objectivity; indeed, their hope is to persuade us to come to faith in Jesus (John 20:30–31). So whenever you encounter different versions of what looks like the same event, the question isn't, "Which one is right?" but rather, "What does this difference tell me about the distinct confession of faith the author is making?" The intentional choices the evangelists make provide clues to their literary and theological aims.

In Matthew, Mark, and Luke, Jesus' cleansing of the Temple by driving out the money changers portrays the rising tension between Jesus and the religious authorities. In fact, Jesus' attack on their sacrificial system is one of the last straws that provoke his opponents to determine to put Jesus to death.

In John, however, the action serves an entirely different literary and theological purpose. At the outset of the Fourth Gospel, John the Baptizer declared that Jesus is "the Lamb of God who takes away the sin of the world" (John 1:29). Further in John's gospel, the day on which Jesus is crucified is the Day of Preparation for the Passover (in the other three accounts that Friday is Passover), which means that Jesus dies at the time when the priests are sacrificing the passover lambs (John 19:31). Jesus, according to John, is the new passover lamb. The very first thing Jesus does in his public ministry, therefore, is to drive out the money changers from the Temple. Why? Because now that God's own passover lamb is among us, there simply is no more need for any more sacrifice.

Scriptural References

Matthew 21:12–13; Mark 11:15–17; 13:1–2; Luke 19:45–46; John 1:29, 2:13–25, 19:31, 20:30–31

Suggested Additional Sources for Reading

- Marcus Borg and John Dominic Crossan, *The Last Week: What the Gospels Really Teach about Jesus' Final Days in Jerusalem* (HarperOne, 2007).
- Marcus Borg and N. T. Wright, *The Meaning of Jesus: Two Visions* (HarperOne, 2007).
- John Dominic Crossan, *Who Killed Jesus?* (HarperSanFrancisco, 1995).
- M. Eugene Boring and Fred B. Craddock, *The People's New Testament Commentary* (Westminster John Knox Press, 2010).
- David Lose, *Making Sense of Scripture* (Augsburg Fortress Press, 2009).
- Enter the Bible: http://www.enterthebible.org.

Suggested Questions for Further Discussion/Thought

1. Does it bother you that the same story seems to take place at two different times within the gospels? Why or why not?
2. Do you feel like today's Christian churches follow the example of Mark, Matthew, and Luke, focusing God's power or holiness on our places of worship, or do we embrace John's notion that the greater body of Christ in the world maintains God's authority?
3. Is it difficult or helpful to think of the gospel writers as rearranging some of the details of the story so as to make a theological confession of faith?

117

34. In Mark 9:37, Jesus says, "Whoever welcomes me welcomes not me but the one who sent me." Is Jesus saying here that he is not actually God?

Brandon Gilvin

Who is...
Brandon Gilvin

I believe a day without breaking a sweat is a day wasted.

Jesus' self-understanding is a hotly debated subject for scholars and people of faith. It is not entirely clear whether or not Jesus saw himself as God Incarnate. Likewise, most of the doctrines and theological understandings of what it meant for Jesus to be divine were worked out well after his death—and the death of the earliest followers.

The debates between Arius and Athanasius are a great case study. Both men understood the divinity of Jesus—and the Christian response that should follow—differently. Both, however, appealed to scriptural proof in ways that were convincing. In the end, Athanasius won the debate (arguing that Jesus was substantially divine from the beginning, whereas Arius argued that Jesus achieved full divinity and union with the Godhead through obedience).

Even this scripture in Mark could be used to buttress an Arian or Athanasian argument. Does the reception of Jesus mean that one receives God fully? Or is it implying a distinction?

I would say, though Athanasius' position is considered orthodox, that an examination of scripture can be used to argue either side of the debate. The gospels and epistles are, after all, narratives and letters written in specific contexts, not systematic theologies meant to explain things for the ages.

Is Jesus saying here that he is not actually God?

R. M. Keelan Downton

Who is...
R. M. Keelan Downton

I'm a huge fan of open source operating systems (but can't quite abandon OSX . . . yet).

A. The first thing to understand is that identifying Messiah/Christ as God was not as important as proclaiming the resurrection as a sign of God's victory over the apparent order of the world. When the church finally gets around to describing the Trinity, it is the fact that Jewish (strictly monotheist) disciples and their successors worshipped Jesus that leads them to conclude that Messiah/Christ must be God or they would all be idolaters.

The second thing to understand is that Jesus brings this up in response to an argument the disciples were having about who was the greatest. It is a powerful statement that the gospel is so contrary to the apparent order of the world that even the Messiah/Christ takes a position of deference. And perhaps more importantly, Jesus draws a straight line between receiving (I thinking "welcoming" works better here) a child and welcoming God. It is the same connection that Jesus is making in the parable of the sheep and the goats: You care for me by caring for the most vulnerable; you encounter me in the concrete realities of human need.

Finally, while this kind of statement leads some people to think of the Trinity in terms of one sending and another being sent, I'm convinced Jesus is actually pointing us toward an understanding of God as the interrelation of mutual deference between three eternal persons that we are invited into, and can begin participating in, only when we let go of our incessant striving to be "the greatest."

David Lose

A. As soon as we talk about Jesus both "being God" and "being sent from God" (and so presumably independent of God, at least God the Father), we venture into the rough-and-tumble terrain of the Trinity. And we'd better get one thing straight: No one *really* understands the Trinity.

But even if we don't fully understand the Trinity, we can still appreciate why it is important. The Trinity conveys that God is, at heart, relational. The doctrine of the Trinity, whatever else it does, conveys that the innermost being and essence of God is relationship, the eternal relationship between God the

119

Father, God the Son, and God the Holy Spirit. So in Jesus—and especially in a verse like Mark 9:37—we have two important promises.

First, God is relational. God sends Jesus. More importantly, God sends Jesus *to us*. So there is the relationship between God the Father (who sends) and God the Son (who is being sent), but now we are invited into that relationship. The Father sends the Son to us in order that we might share in this relationship.

Second, what we see in Jesus is what we get in God. This is important because, as John relates, "No one has ever seen God" (John 1:18a). This can make God seem mysterious, unknowable, and even frightening. What is God ultimately like? Is God reliable? The clues we might discern from nature—that range from beautiful sunsets to volcanoes—are ambiguous at best. But Jesus promises (here we are back at the Trinity) that to know and receive Jesus is to know and receive the one who sent him. Or to borrow from John once more, "It is God the only Son, who is close to the Father's heart, who has made him known" (John 1:18b).

Scriptural References

Mark 9:37; John 1:18

Suggested Additional Sources for Reading

- Marcus J. Borg and N. T. Wright, *The Meaning of Jesus: Two Visions* (HarperOne, 2007).
- Paula Fredriksen, *From Jesus to Christ: The Origins of the New Testament Images of Jesus* (Yale Univ. Press, 2000).

Suggested Questions for Further Discussion/Thought

1. How do both Jesus' divinity and humanity affect your faith?
2. How do you see the expressions of the Trinity interrelated with each other?
3. Is there a risk of idolatry in focusing too much on the worship of Jesus?

Question

35. Aside from the women and the disciples, are there any recorded stories of personal interaction between Jesus and other people after he was resurrected? Why wouldn't he appear to more people? And why did he stay on Earth for forty days? Is that symbolically important?

Amy Reeder Worley

The resurrection stories in the Bible are inconsistent. For example, in the gospel resurrection stories Jesus only appears to the women and the disciples. However Paul, who wrote closest in time to Jesus' crucifixion, says Jesus "appeared to more than five hundred brothers and sisters at one time" and to Paul, who was not a disciple (1 Corinthians 15:3–8).

So how should we understand such inconsistencies? Some Christians attempt to reconcile the different resurrection accounts so they can read them as literally true. For me, there are too many differences in these stories for a literal reconciliation to make sense. But what if we look at them as a metaphor?

A metaphor is not some linguistic trick that clouds the literal truth. Rather it conveys in words an idea greater than the words themselves. In the same way the symbol of the cross means more to Christians than a Roman torture device, the resurrection stories convey more meaning than just the literal words.

The reference to Jesus remaining on Earth for forty days is our first clue that these accounts are metaphorical. Forty is a significant biblical symbol. It rained for forty days during the flood (Genesis 7:12). Moses spent forty days on the mount two times (Exodus 34: 28–29; Deuteronomy 10:10). The Israelites wondered in the wilderness for forty years (Exodus 16:35). Elijah walked forty days to Mount Horeb (1 Kings 19:8). Jesus fasted and prayed for forty days in the wilderness (Matthew 4:2). In all of these accounts, "forty" signifies a time of contemplation and hardship before a spiritual revelation.

During the forty days before the ascension the disciples probably struggled to understand Jesus' death within the context of his life. Then, in various ways, they had spiritual experiences of the resurrected Jesus, which renewed their hope. As Paul explains, "What is sown is perishable. What is raised is imperishable . . . It is sown in a physical body, it is raised in a spiritual body" (1 Corinthians 15:26–44).

121

Thus after forty days of struggle and contemplation, the Spirit of Christ was revealed and the cornerstone of Christianity was made manifest. Metaphors often contain truths too large for words. I can think of no better example than the resurrection stories.

Mark Van Steenwyk

Who is...
Mark Van Steenwyk

I used to be painfully shy.

It seems fishy to people that Jesus only appeared to his closest followers—the eleven disciples (Judas left the group to betray Jesus and kill himself) and a few faithful women (including Mary Magdalene and Mary). Folks have speculated that Christianity was invented by a small group of people who wanted to have power over a bunch of superstitious rubes. But there were others who saw the risen Jesus.

In Luke 24, he appeared to two people walking from Jerusalem to Emmaus.

The Apostle Paul claims to have encountered the risen Jesus on the road to Damascus (Acts 9).

Paul also claims that five hundred believers (including Jesus' brother, James) saw Jesus all at once (1 Corinthians 15).

So if we take these claims at face value, over five hundred people saw Jesus after he was resurrected. There may have been more. We don't know. And at least two of them, Paul and James, weren't followers of Jesus until they encountered him postresurrection.

It seems that, within weeks of Jesus' resurrection, the movement had grown from dozens to the low thousands. If the whole thing was based on the lies made up by a dozen people behind closed doors, you'd think it would take a lot longer to kick things off.

It seems to me that Jesus' appearance to five hundred people was enough to get things going. Furthermore, there didn't seem to be many people running around trying to expose the conspiracy.

So then, why didn't Jesus appear to even more? He could have revealed himself to millions! Keep in mind that while Jesus is risen, he can't be in more than one place at a time apart from the presence of the Holy Spirit. He was still one guy, and he only had forty days. It seems to me that he took that time to be with his closest friends, preparing them to continue his work.

Why forty days? I suppose it is because "forty" is a biblical number of testing or preparation. There were forty days of rain for Noah. Forty days on Mount Sinai for Moses. Forty years of wandering before the people could enter the promised land. Forty days of temptation by the devil for Jesus. Jesus spent forty days with us before ascending to his Father. It was his preparation, and it was, in a way, a time of preparation for his disciples.

Brandon Gilvin

Who is...
Brandon Gilvin

I want to someday write an article on 1980s graphic novels, apocalyptic literature, and the end of the Cold War.

A. There are several stories of postresurrection appearances.
The Secret Book of James, a "lost" piece of Christian literature found with the Nag Hammadi scrolls in 1945, records a private postresurrection revelation to James and Peter. Likewise, he appears to James in the gospel of the Hebrews, a book of which we have no copy, that is quoted multiple times by early church leaders.

Curiously, in the Book of Mormon (3 Nephi 11), Jesus appears to the indigenous people of the Americas.

Unless you are a Latter-Day Saint, none of these books is canonical.

Literarily and theologically, it doesn't make sense for a resurrected Jesus to appear to someone who did not know of him before the crucifixion. The point of the gospels is to show that the early church experienced God's presence in the life and ministry of Jesus. This experience was so powerful that the early church continued to experience God's grace through Jesus even after he died and felt compelled to proclaim Jesus' defeat of death (whether it is historical or not) as a sign of God's imminent reign.

There is, of course, one key exception to this—Saul/Paul.

Paul, who eloquently recounted his experience with the resurrected Christ, had no firsthand experience with the historical Jesus. Whether or not this was a historically verifiable experience or highly metaphorical language to explain a completely new understanding of reality for Paul, however, is a question that depends on your perspective.

The forty-day timeline is also likely a literary invention. It is an oft-repeated phrase throughout the Bible that indicates a complete cycle.

Scriptural References

Genesis 7:12; Exodus 16:35; 34: 28–29; Deuteronomy 10:10; 1 Kings 19:8; Matthew 4:2; 1 Corinthians 15:3–8; 15:26–44

Suggested Additional Sources for Reading

- John Buehrens, *Understanding the Bible: An Introduction for Skeptics, Seekers, and Religious Liberals* (Beacon Press, 2003).
- John Dominic Crossan, *The Birth of Christianity* (HarperSanFrancisco, 1998).
- R. C. Symes, "The Resurrection Myths about Jesus: A Progressive Christian Interpretation," http://www.religioustolerance.org/symes01.htm.
- Joseph Smith Jr., *The Book of Mormon: Another Testament of Jesus Christ.*
- Bart Ehrman, *Lost Scriptures: Books That Did Not Make It into the New Testament* (Oxford Univ. Press, 2003).
- Robert Miller, *The Complete Gospels* (Polebridge, 1995).

Suggested Questions for Further Discussion/Thought

1. Is reading the resurrection metaphorically somehow heretical?
2. Does a metaphorical reading of scripture mean that you don't believe Jesus physically rose from the dead?
3. Do the factual inconsistencies in the biblical passages impact the truthfulness of them?

36. Was Jesus ever sick? If so, why not just heal himself?

Mark Van Steenwyk

A. Jesus wasn't a wizard. He didn't have a storehouse of magic that he could use on whim. Rather Jesus is, in a very strange and real sense, God. Everything Jesus does now, and did when he walked among us, was done to reveal the kingdom of God. Everything was an act of love.

Let's just grant, for the sake of argument, that Jesus got sick. If that were the case, I doubt very much he would have healed himself—unless, of course, it was the sort of situation that would have stopped him from accomplishing his mission. What if he had gotten trapped in an elephant stampede and his body got crushed into putty? Would his last thoughts have been "Father, it looks like you'll have to have a *second* only begotten son?" or would he have healed himself instantly by saying "in my own name, be healed"?

I don't know. I'm not sure I really want to venture a serious guess. The more interesting question is "was Jesus ever sick?" I think he did get sick. Jesus was as human as we are. He was *more* than human, but still human. He stubbed his toe. He tripped over stuff. He got the flu. He was susceptible to injury and even death.

That he could experience all of these things doesn't make him any less remarkable, rather it simply makes the fact that he was also God all the more remarkable. God, it would seem, got diarrhea. God caught a cold. God felt—and feels—the limitations of our humanity.

Joan Ball

Who is...
Joan Ball

I am a college professor, but my undergraduate cumulative average was a 2.25.

A. I have no idea whether or not Jesus was sick. I can't recall reading about sickness in scripture. That said, there isn't much discussion of Jesus bathing, sleeping, eating, or blowing his nose either. I find that speculating about this kind of thing makes for long trips down dark rabbit holes, so I will abstain.

Peter J. Walker

We don't know if Jesus was ever sick, but we do know Jesus was tired (John 4:6), saddened (Luke 13:34), angry (Matthew 3:7), grieved (John 11:38), and terrified (Matthew 26:39). "This man of sorrows" experienced everything about being human because he was human. So it wouldn't be surprising to find he was down with the flu or a migraine from time to time. But to supernaturally heal himself, Jesus would have undermined his own resistance to temptation in the desert. He didn't help himself in the desert, and he didn't save himself on the cross. Jesus' life was characterized by giving himself for others, even unto death. Intermittently healing himself would seem to run contrary to this ethos of self-sacrifice.

Today, it's informative to walk into a Christian bookstore and browse the wall of best sellers: Why wouldn't we expect Jesus to heal himself? We have created a religious culture in which personal improvement, wellness, and success are the natural by-products of Christianity. While self-healing, Jesus should probably be giving himself a total money makeover, developing his personal mission statement, and selling vitamins via multilevel marketing.

In Matthew 5, Jesus lists groups of people who are blessed: "[B]lessed are the poor in spirit . . . blessed are those who mourn . . . blessed are the meek." Jesus is turning prevailing logic on its head: The fortunate aren't the only ones blessed by God. The implications of this are daunting. Jesus said, "For the gate is narrow and the road is hard that leads to life, and there are few who find it" (Matthew 7:14).

The way of Jesus is not only countercultural, it is counterintuitive. It asks us to die our best death when the world invites us to live our best life.

Scriptural References

Matthew 3:7; 7:14; 26:39; Luke 13:34; John 4:6; 11:38

Suggested Additional Sources for Reading

- Brian D. McLaren, *The Secret Message of Jesus* (Thomas Nelson, 2007).
- Henri Nouwen, *Reaching Out* (Doubleday, 1975).
- Thomas Merton, *No Man Is an Island* (Harcourt, Brace, 1955).

Suggested Questions for Further Discussion/Thought

1. Does Jesus seem less special if he could, somehow, get sick?
2. Why do we assume that Jesus would be incapable of getting sick?

3. In what ways have you suffered in your life? How has that suffering informed your view of yourself and of God?
4. How have you been blessed in your life? Have you grown more through blessings or suffering?
5. Should the Christian life lead to an easier life?

37. After Jesus' baptism, he is tempted in the desert several times. How is this different from when he teaches in Matthew 5:28 that "everyone who looks at a woman with lust has already committed adultery with her in his heart"? Aren't these basically the same thing?

Becky Garrison

Who is...
Becky Garrison

After having been raised by hippie parents, I went all Alex P. Keaton and joined the Young Republicans in my twenties.

In the desert, Satan tried to get Jesus to follow him by appealing to his physical humanity by offering him bread. When that failed, he tried to force Jesus to perform a miracle as though he was some trained devotional doggie who could use the power given to him by God at will. After Jesus blew him off, Satan tried unsuccessfully to lure him in by promising a kingdom here on earth. While these three options must have been mighty tempting, Jesus didn't let these temptations enter his heart and influence his thinking.

Compare that to a man who might claim he's not sinning because he's not doing the dirty deed. But his mind is corrupted because he keeps thinking about doing the dirty deed with another dude's lady. While someone in a relationship might not be having an actual affair by sending steamy e-mails, flirting on Facebook, and posting titillating tweets to another party, they've definitely crossed into that gray area where commandments might not be actually broken, but boundaries were definitely crossed.

Phil Snider

Who is...
Phil Snider

For someone who can't sing, I do a great impression of Johnny Cash.

A. In the highly controversial film *The Last Temptation of Christ*, Jesus imagines what life might be like if he chose a path that didn't lead to the cross but instead to a comfortable family life. This is similar to the temptation that many people still face today. While such temptations aren't necessarily relegated to the choice of dying on a cross or raising a family, the basic idea still remains; certain risks are involved when one chooses to follow the call that God places on one's life, and most of us tend to prefer a more comfortable life instead. The temptations that Jesus faced in the desert serve as an overture to Jesus' entire ministry, for they symbolically emphasize the ways that he—in contrast to most of us—refused a comfortable life in order to be faithful to his calling, no matter the consequence.

This is very different from what takes place in Matthew 5:28. In this passage, Jesus is highlighting the dignity of women, implying that they should be treated as human beings and not mere objects. Jesus' words in Matthew 5—combined with several of his other teachings—provocatively challenge the customs and laws of the times, so much so that religious and political authorities wanted to take action in order to get rid of him. Yet he refused to give in, no matter the consequence. So you might say that the story of Jesus' temptation in the desert is connected to Matthew 5:28 but not in the way this question implies.

Joan Ball

Who is...
Joan Ball

I went to the US Air Force Academy (for a year).

A. When tempting Jesus in the desert, Satan went out of his way to create scenarios that would distract and confuse. This was an active and malevolent effort on the part of Satan meant to sideline Jesus and insult the Father. Jesus faced each challenge prayerfully, intelligently, and with self-control and, as a result, Satan was foiled.

For the second scenario to be the same, this generic woman in Matthew must be cast in the role of malicious "temptress" (i.e., Satan). But Jesus know how to seek God, engage the Spirit, and grow in self-control (i.e., not look at the woman lustfully). I'm not buying it. God is bigger than the male libido.

Lee C. Camp

Who is...
Lee C. Camp

I won the State of Alabama Future Farmers of America Public Speaking contest as a junior in high school.

Though it is often assumed that Jesus' temptations in the wilderness entailed a period of intense testing with the "lust of the flesh, lust of the eye, and the vain-glorious pride of life," numerous New Testament scholars these days believe that the temptation in the wilderness was concerned with *what sort of Messiah* Jesus was going to be.

Nonetheless, it seems a fair and important question to ask the difference between a "temptation" and a "lustful thought"? If a man looks at a woman and thinks a lustful thought, has he as much as committed adultery? But perhaps a more helpful question is to ask this: What is the function or purpose of the Sermon on the Mount? Therein Jesus provides a description of a way of life oriented toward the kingdom of heaven. What does it look like to live life in the kingdom of heaven that has come among us, that has invaded human history?

The Beatitudes announce, for example, that the presence of the kingdom entails comfort to the oppressed and the poor and the persecuted faithful. Then the six "antitheses" ("you have heard it said, but I say") announce certain skills or practices that characterize life in the kingdom: reconciliation with estranged parties, rooting out any form of objectification or lust, chastity and preservation of marriage vows, speaking the truth without obfuscation, overcoming evil with good, and doing good to one's enemies. These are holistic, lifestyle, and community-embraced practices, not merely new legalistic rules.

One last note, as Martin Luther once said with regard to temptation and tempting thoughts, we cannot control what birds fly over our heads. We can only control whether they build nests in our hair.

Scriptural References

Matthew 4:1–11; 8:18–20; 10:34–39; 16:24–26; Luke 6:46–49; Galatians 5:22–23

Suggested Additional Sources for Reading

- C. S. Lewis, *The Screwtape Letters* (G. Bless, 1942).
- M. Scott Peck, *People of the Lie* (Simon and Schuster, 1983).
- N. T. Wright, *After You Believe* (HarperOne, 2010).
- Nikos Kazantzakis, trans. P. A. Bien, *The Last Temptation of Christ* (Simon and Schuster, 1960).
- Russell Connors and Patrick McCormick, *Character, Choices, and Community* (Paulist Press, 1998).
- Shane Claiborne, *The Irresistible Revolution* (Zondervan, 2006).

Suggested Questions for Further Discussion/Thought

1. What does it mean to be faithful in a relationship from a Christian perspective?
2. Do you ever feel tension in relationship to what God is calling you to do and the consequences this might have on your life? Is it possible to balance this calling with your personal, vocational, or family life? Why or why not?
3. Do you think Jesus faced the same kind of temptations that most of us face? How so?
4. Do you understand temptation to be an external force or a being (like Satan) in the universe, or is it only found within us humans?

38. In several places in the gospels, Jesus suggests that even he doesn't know when he will return again to earth. Why not? Is God keeping it a secret from him? And if Jesus actually is God, shouldn't he know everything?

Phil Snider

A lot of times, we want to make God out to be a kind of supreme rational intellect ruling over the cosmos—a God who knows everything and can do anything. From this perspective, it's only logical to think that if Jesus was God then he should have access to the mind of God and, thus, know when he will return again to earth.

But what if we view God not as a noun but rather as a verb? What if we view God not so much as a grand being ruling over the cosmos, but rather as the power of love that emanates from below? What if the God aspect of Jesus' life wasn't so much about knowledge, might, and truth, but rather about compassion, love, and vulnerability? In that case, Jesus' lack of knowledge doesn't necessarily diminish his connection to the Divine.

Furthermore, what if the revelation of God given in Jesus is a radically different revelation from what we usually expect? Indeed, one of the great paradoxes of the Trinity is that Jesus reveals God most fully to us when Jesus is most fully human (one might recall that in the gospels, Jesus often refers to himself as the "Son of man," which can be translated as the "human one"). With that in mind, what if the revelation of God disclosed in Jesus is not a revelation of a supreme rational intellect that knows everything, but rather a power of love, compassion and grace that changes everything?

Tripp Fuller

Who is...
Tripp Fuller
I still listen to '80s hair metal.

It is essential to always remember that Jesus is not absent from Earth. He promises to be present in the celebration of communion, and he told us that when we care for the least of these, we do so to him. Not only that, but the church in all its diversity is Christ's body, here on Earth now. Right now we have a mission to celebrate what God has done in Christ, invite others to the Jesus' table, and join God in creating a more just and loving world. The risen Christ is in our midst and calling us today to get busy!

Jesus, like us, was human and knew that history was a stricken with contingency. The future was not complete in all its details but the process includes our real choices. That the man Jesus didn't know the exact plan for the future shouldn't be surprising, but what shouldn't be missed is that he was confident in the future. Jesus was always confident that the kingdom of God was already in the business of coming and that when it fully arrived, God would set the Earth to right so that God's just will is done on Earth as in heaven. His confidence was not in a clock counting down like a New Year's party but rather in the God he knew as *Abba*.

Jesus had confidence in the future because of who God is. The God he fully trusted with the future is the same one we are called to trust. Like Jesus, we can see this trust playing out in our lives. Unlike Jesus, who is the image of the invisible God, we fail to do this all the time. In those moments, we can take comfort knowing that we are part of the larger body of Christ, forgiven yet sinners with a call to join in God's coming.

Pablo A. Jiménez

A. This question presupposes an idea foreign to the Bible, destiny. For some reason, popular culture believes that the future is totally mapped out, that all future events have already a date in which to occur.

The concept of destiny is popular in literature and its correlates: drama and film. It offers a narrative backdrop to the action. Destiny pulls the story toward the future and bends the will of all characters.

However, the Bible has little use for the concept of destiny. For example, the Hebrew Scriptures tell how the prophet Isaiah tells king Hezekiah that he will die shortly (Isaiah 38:1). However, God extends the king's life in response to his prayers (Isaiah 38:2–8). Notice how the prophecy changes according to the will of God.

Revelation stresses the same point when it says that the risen Christ has "the keys of Death and of Hades" (Revelation 1:18). Once again, the Bible stresses that the future is in God's hands.

Jesus chastises his disciples' curiosity in Acts 1:7, saying, "It is not for you to know the times or periods that the Father has set by his own authority." The text does not say that God has set a date for the final judgment. Interpreted in light of the previous texts, Jesus says that God will "restore the kingdom" (Acts 1:6) whenever God deems it correct. The future is open to God's divine will.

Scriptural References

Isaiah 38:1–8; Acts 1:6–8; 2 Corinthians 12:9; Philippians 2:1–11; Revelation 1:18

Suggested Additional Sources for Reading

- Douglas John Hall, *The Cross in Our Context* (Fortress Press, 2003).
- John Caputo, *The Weakness of God* (Indiana Univ. Press, 2006).
- Carter Heyward, *Saving Jesus from Those Who Are Right* (Fortress Press, 1999).

Suggested Questions for Further Discussion/Thought

1. When you think about God, do you think primarily in terms of sheer power or unconditional love? Are these images of God mutually exclusive?
2. What might it mean to say that God's love qualifies God's power?
3. When the gospel writers wrote about Jesus' return to earth, were they talking about the same thing as the rapture? Why or why not?
4. Is knowledge the same thing as power?

39. Did Jesus believe God wanted him to be crucified? If so, why did he ask God, "My Father, if it is possible, let this cup pass from me" in the garden of Gethsemane?

Jarrod McKenna

Who is...
Jarrod McKenna

Marx Brothers films are underrated.

A. There is a stunning image from the Tiananmen Square uprising in 1989. A lone student places himself in front of the rolling war machines of one of the world's largest oppressive superpowers. Armed only with what looks like a bag and a vision of the future, he refuses to be passive and steps out, allowing the possibility of history and hope to clash over his body.

Burnt into our collective memory is this fragile symbol of democracy on a collision course with the Communist government's power. What would the night before this action be like for him? Did this student have a sense of vocation that his life would be given to open up a new reality for his people?

Our Lord Jesus is not less human than this warrior whose only weapon was unarmed truth. And Jesus didn't do less than what the student did in taking an oppressive empire. On the cross, Jesus took on all evil, and all empires, exhausting their worst in his very body and astonishingly responds with "Father, forgive them for they do not know what they are doing" (Luke 23:34).

Jesus in the garden prays what any one of us would pray for, another way other than the pain of confrontational suffering love. Jesus prays in the garden (Matthew 26:39, 42) as he taught his disciples to pray (Matthew 6:9–13) "your will be done" and in doing so goes to the cross, bringing the coming kingdom on Earth as it is in heaven. In taking upon himself the suffering that initiates the end of all suffering, Jesus does not simply do the will of God; Jesus *is* the will of God.

Joan Ball

A. I believe Jesus' request was a prayer for mercy. He knew the pain and suffering that lay before him, and he was willing to take it to the bitter end. Being fully human and fully divine, he engaged his humanity by engaging in prayer and petition to ask the Father if there was another way.

135

Did Jesus believe God wanted him to be crucified?

While modern western Christians have created a culture where questioning God is often viewed as a lack of faithfulness, Jesus was a Jew. Questioning, negotiating, and wrestling with God was not only acceptable, it was—and still is—a critical part of the faith tradition. To cry out to the Father was in keeping with the example set by king David and the Old Testament prophets underscoring the notion that we can question God and be faithful to God in the same breath.

R. M. Keelan Downton

It doesn't take any prophetic powers for a leader who is attracting large crowds with teachings that challenge the authority of both the religious and the political establishments to conclude that continuing to do so will likely result in death.

If you start from the perspective of Jesus having access to the full knowledge of God, the Gethsemane prayer is inherently confusing: Jesus knows it's important that he be crucified but asks if God could work it out some other way. From this perspective, "your will be done" is a fatalistic resignation to suffering—a perspective that has been immensely destructive in the history of the church, particularly to women.

If Jesus is only working from knowledge of the likely outcome, it means that Jesus prayed out of the same struggle we face: embodying love and justice in the face of loss and uncertainty. "Let this cup pass" is a real search for a creative solution beyond what circumstances suggest will happen. From this perspective, "your will be done" means participating in the intentions of God for the world, even when those in power oppose those intentions.

The suffering perpetuated by Roman torturers is not intended to set out suffering as an ideal, but rather serves as the radical sign that those who resist God by inflicting suffering on others cannot win. Their actions are truly horrific and yet insufficient to prevent the ultimate victory of God the gospel invites us to participate in.

Lee C. Camp

Who is...
Lee C. Camp

I dislike much of southern religion but enjoy much of southern culture, including fried chicken and biscuits, bluegrass, and the Ryman Auditorium.

A. The four gospels indicate a purposeful intentionality in Jesus' moving toward Jerusalem. Jesus seems quite aware that this would entail his own crucifixion. What could the prayer in the Garden mean, then? The synoptic gospels each recount Jesus' temptation experience in the wilderness at the beginning of his ministry. Many times, these temptations are understood to be a reference to the "lust of the flesh, lust of the eye, and the vain-glorious pride of life," a way of saying that Jesus was simply tempted in all points like as we are.

But more likely, the temptation accounts raise a different concern: *What sort of messiah will Jesus be?* A welfare king, who puts a car in every garage and a chicken in every pot? A religious reformer, who makes a great spectacle in the Temple and sets right matters of a proper religious cult once and for all? Or will he be a mighty emperor, ruling over all lands through imperialistic might?

From that point forward, Jesus set out to be a very different sort of messiah, one who shall save the world through suffering love. When in Mark 8, for example, Jesus teaches the twelve that his being "Son of Man" will entail abuse and mocking and death, Peter rebukes Jesus: "Do not say such a thing, Jesus! You are the Messiah, and no Messiah should face such." Jesus' response is instructive: "Get behind me, Satan." That is, Peter has voiced the same temptation Jesus faced in the wilderness: Go be a conquering messiah, not a suffering one.

Then in the final hours before the crucifixion, Jesus faces the temptation again: Must this really be the way? Is there no other? May I not call ten thousand angels to vanquish evil?

David Lose

A. The testimony of the early church to Jesus—including what Jesus *knew* about his crucifixion—is both rich and varied. Jesus' prayer to "let this cup pass" is in Matthew, Mark, and Luke—called the "synoptic" (Greek for "seen together") gospels because they are the most similar. In John's gospel, by contrast, Jesus not only shows no such moment of weakness, but when Peter attempts to defend him by the sword, Jesus asks the opposite question: "Am I *not* to drink the cup that the Father has given me?" (John 18:11).

137

At this point, we therefore have two options: Either try to decide which of the gospel accounts was "right," or listen carefully for the distinct confession of faith that each gospel writer offers. In the case of the prayer in the synoptic gospels, two theological confessions come to the fore. First, Jesus is *like us* and so experiences these events as we might experience them. Who wouldn't be anxious regarding the impending struggle, suffering, and death the cross represents? Second, Jesus is *faithful*. Whatever human fear Jesus displays, he is nevertheless faithful to his father, to his mission, and to us. Hence his prayer continues, "[Y]et not what I want, but what you want" (Mark 14:36).

So there you have it. Jesus is really *like* us, and therefore understands the challenges and struggles we endure. And Jesus is really *for* us, committed to us enough that he would suffer and die on the cross. Not a bad set of confessions to hang on to when you, yourself, feel stretched beyond your limits.

Scriptural References

Genesis 32:24–31; Matthew 6:9–13; 26:36–42; Mark 14:32–42; Luke 22:39–46

Suggested Additional Sources for Reading

- Watchman Nee, *The Normal Christian Life* (Victory Press, 1963).
- John Howard Yoder, *The Politics of Jesus* (Eerdmans, 1972).
- John Howard Yoder, *The Original Revolution* (Herald Press, 1972).
- David Lose, *Making Sense of Scripture* (Augsburg Fortress Press, 2009).
- David Lose, *Making Sense of the Christian Faith* (Augsburg Fortress Press, 2010).
- N. T. Wright, *The Challenge of Jesus* (IVP, 2011).
- Christopher D. Marshall, *Beyond Retribution* (Eerdmans, 2001).

Suggested Questions for Further Discussion/Thought

1. What does it mean to you to know that Jesus was afraid like we can be? Does it mean that Jesus understands our fears because he has experienced fear firsthand?
2. Why are verses that insist Jesus has control of his own destiny (Mark 14:35, 41; Matthew 26:55; Luke 22:14) so important?
3. Why is it important that we don't think God wills suffering but sometimes calls us to a suffering that exposes the systems that make others suffer?
4. Orthodox Christianity affirms that Jesus is fully human (as human as you) and fully divine (as divine as the Holy Spirit and the Father). Why is it that some Christians focus on one and neglect the other?

uestion

40. Was Jesus ever wrong? About what?

Sherri Emmons

Who is...
Sherri Emmons

I'm addicted to Facebook.

A. If we take seriously the concept that Jesus was both fully human and fully divine, then we have to accept that he made mistakes. To be human is to make mistakes. This human side of Christ is what draws me to Christianity. Knowing that Christ suffered the way we do tells me that he understands our doubts, our mistakes, and our suffering in a way no purely divine being could.

We see evidence of Jesus' humanity in his need to withdraw from the crowds, his impatience with his disciples, his anger at the moneylenders in the temple, and his pleading with God in the garden of Gethsemane. And we have one endearing example of misbehavior when Jesus as a child stays behind at the Temple after his parents have left, which certainly must have worried Mary and Joseph out of their wits. Talking with the elders was fine, but he was wrong not to tell his parents where he was.

Joan Ball

A. On first blush, this question looked a lot like the question about whether Jesus had ever been sick—subject to speculation only. But as I considered the question further, the story of Jesus clearing the Temple in Jerusalem, which shows up in each of the gospels, kept coming to mind. While I am not in a position to say whether Jesus' decision to enter that courtyard and kick over the tables was right or wrong (way over my pay grade), I do know that it is a scripture that is used frequently as an excuse for unloving, aggressive behavior among Christians.

Too often we allow Christians behaving badly to call biblical principles into question, and I will not do that here. I just wonder how Jesus would feel about the holy anger and aggression that has been justified in the name of the events of that day.

R. M. Keelan Downton

A. This question appears to be about things that Jesus asserted or denied, but in reality it is about how the person answering positions her or himself in relation to Jesus—a question of loyalty and trust.

There are some trivial anomalies like where Jesus says he won't go up to a particular feast but then a few days later he does. But these are a distraction.

What matters is whether I choose to arrange my life to match the teachings of Jesus or not. To the extent that I do, I affirm loyalty to Jesus as Messiah/Christ who can be fully trusted. To the extent that I arrange my life in different ways, I assert that Jesus was wrong and express loyalty only to my own decision-making process.

Scriptural References

Matthew 4:13, 21:11–13; 21:12–17, 23–27; 26:36–46; Mark 11:15–19, 27–33 14:32–42; Luke 2:39–52; 19:45–48, 20:1–8; John 2:13–16

Suggested Additional Sources for Reading

- Brennan Manning, *The Furious Longing of God* (David C. Cook, 2009).
- Peter Scazzero, *The Emotionally Healthy Church* (Zondervan, 2003).
- Charlotte Allen, *The Human Christ: Search for the Historical Jesus* (Free Press, 1998).
- Robert W. Funk, *The Five Gospels: What Did Jesus Really Say? The Search for the Authentic Words of Jesus* (Macmillan, 1993).
- Marcus J. Borg, *Reading the Bible Again for the First Time: Taking the Bible Seriously but Not Literally* (HarperSanFrancisco, 2001).

Suggested Questions for Further Discussion/Thought

1. Does it compromise Jesus' ministry in any way if he ever was wrong? How?
2. There are accounts throughout the Old Testament of God changing his mind; does this imply that God can be wrong?
3. If we believe Jesus may have been wrong on occasion, how might this challenge our confidence in his vision for his own ministry?

41. Some gospel accounts trace Jesus' lineage to King David through Mary's family, while others trace it through Joseph. Is one of these wrong? And why trace it through Joseph if he wasn't Jesus' father by blood?

Pablo A. Jiménez

Who is...
Pablo A. Jiménez

I have written more than twenty books, most of them in Spanish.

A. Once again, here our modern sensitivity clashes with ancient thought. Modern western thought tends to be linear and exclusive, while ancient biblical thought tends to be circular and inclusive. For example, Egyptian mythology has several versions of the creation account. Each version explains an aspect of creation, not the whole. Most of these versions contradict the others; they do not match. However, Egyptians saw no need of picking one over the other. The idea of having a single comprehensive and truthful account is a modern concern, not an ancient one.

In the case of Jesus' genealogy, several scholars understand that Matthew traces his lineage through the maternal line (Matthew 1:1–17). However, Luke 3:23–38 traces Jesus genealogy through Joseph's family. The explanation is rather simple. Matthew follows the Jewish tradition and Luke follows Greek conventions. Jewish lineage was usually traced through the mother, given that there were no reliable paternity tests. In biblical times, the son of a Gentile man and a Jewish woman was Jewish, while the daughter of a Gentile woman and a Jewish man was Gentile.

However, Luke writes to a mostly Gentile audience that would have frowned upon the idea of having a lineage traced through the mother.

Brandon Gilvin

Who is...
Brandon Gilvin

I'm a nerd.

A. Genealogies in the gospels were not produced in an attempt to record history in a precise way. The tracing of Jesus' lineage is done in order to make a theological, not a historical, point. The gospel of Luke (3:23–38) traces Jesus' ancestry through Joseph (though it includes an interesting, ambiguous little phrase in verse 23 about Joseph's paternity), and traces it through a number of patriarchs pulled straight from the TaNaK[20] (Genesis 5, 11; Ruth 4; 1 Chronicles 1 and 2), and ends by tracing it all the way to Adam, the first man. In Luke's account, Jesus is connected to the birth of humanity, and thus connected to all who are born.

Matthew, however, traces Jesus' ancestry back to Abraham, God's partner in covenant (Genesis 12). Special focus is placed on David. Note, too, that while Matthew mentions several women, the lineage is traced through Joseph, not Mary. Again, this highlights some of the key figures in the TaNaK, all of whom played critical roles in the maintenance of the covenant between Israel and God. Jesus fits prominently into that covenant—and the genealogy concludes by emphasizing that point . . . twice (Matthew 1:16, 17).

The fact is—we cannot prove either of these historically. Therefore, we can't truly say one is wrong. Instead, it is important to read them as part of two independent tellings of Jesus' life and ministry, both of which proclaim the presence of God in the life of Jesus but draw different conclusions about how and why that happened, and what it means for the reader.

Scriptural References

Genesis 5, 11, 12; Ruth 4; 1 Chronicles 1–2; Matthew 1:1–17; Luke 3:23–38

Suggested Additional Source for Reading

- Raymond Edward Brown, *The Birth of the Messiah: A Commentary on the Infancy Narratives in the Gospels of Matthew and Luke* (Yale Univ. Press, 1999).

---

20. Acronym for Jewish Canon: The Torah (Law) Nevi'im (Prophets) and Ketuvim (Writings).

- Russell Pregeant, *Matthew: Chalice Commentaries for Today* (Chalice Press, 2004).
- O. Wesley Allen, *Reading the Synoptic Gospels: Basic Methods for Interpreting Matthew, Mark, and Luke* (Chalice Press, 2000).

Suggested Questions for Further Discussion/Thought

1. Why do the circumstances of Jesus' birth matter?
2. If Jesus' birth were neither miraculous nor tied to these historical figures, would he still be important? Divine?
3. Does the suggestion that different books of the Bible account for things as significant as Jesus' ancestry differently have any effect on your value of scripture? Why or why not?

42. Did Jesus study other religions? Which ones?

Jarrod McKenna

Who is...
Jarrod McKenna

I have the most wonderful wife and son and community that make it possible for me to receive and seek to live God's love.

Those who like to speculate about Jesus jet-setting (or donkey-setting?) to India to study Buddhism then coming back enlightened at the age of thirty to share his findings are not just completely barren when it comes to any scrap of historical evidence; they are bordering on anti-Semitism to believe that Jesus' own Jewish tradition could not produce him. Those who don't understand the Jewishness of Jesus will fail to understand the universally inclusive eschatological Judaism that the apostle Paul is advocating in the New Testament. Sadly this good news of ancient Israel's hope realized in the nonviolent Messiah Jesus is lost on many Christians.

Jesus is not just a student of Judaism who is suggesting a few revisions; he is the fulfillment of the Jewish hope. This hope was not for some privatized escapist fantasy of our "spirits" fleeing matter to hang out on clouds with fat, winged babies apt at playing the harp. This hope is that in history, God's self-revelation and reign would break in decisively, bringing deliverance, justice, healing, and peace replacing slavery, injustice, suffering, and violence.

In our Lord Jesus' deep education in Torah and the Prophets (particularly Isaiah) he sensed a unique vocation to do for Israel what only God could do. Jesus as the Suffering Servant (Isaiah 53) becomes the true Israel, and by doing so, reveals the true God. God in Christ substitutes our exile, oppression, injustice, and evil for the healing justice, delivering peace, and saving joy in the intimacy of God's very presence.

Christian Piatt

Who is...
Christian Piatt

My middle name is Damien.

Jesus grew up, lived, and died a Jewish man; it was only those who followed him later as the movement that came to be known as the early church that were actually known first as Christians.

Though we're not sure if Jesus studied other faiths, he certainly knew something of other beliefs, as is suggested by certain references throughout his ministry. Generally, it seemed that he was alluding to images or concepts the people with whom he was speaking could relate to.

There are parallels between Jesus' message and those in other faiths. In his book *Living Buddha, Living Christ*, Thich Nhat Hanh draws parallels between Jesus and Buddha, not arguing so much that Jesus studied Buddhism but pointing out that there are more similarities than differences in many areas. Marcus Borg offers a more Western perspective in his book *Jesus and Buddha: The Parallel Sayings*. And there are many others on the subject.

Perhaps more interesting than this, though, is how other faiths perceive Jesus. Though traditional Judaism (with the exception of Messianic Judaism) does not understand Jesus to be the Messiah, they do recognize him as an important prophet. And in the Baha'i faith and Islam, he is seen as both a prophet and as the Messiah.

It would be difficult for Jesus never to encounter other faiths in his studies, though it was also very uncommon for people of his era to travel more than a hundred miles or so from their place of birth in a lifetime. Perhaps the most likely truth is that many faiths have arrived at values and beliefs that are found throughout the greater human experience but translated through different cultural, theological, and historical filters. In a sense, this perspective gives even greater significance to the biblical phrase "seek and you shall find."

Phil Snider

A. With few exceptions, scholars agree that Jesus was deeply rooted in first-century Jewish thought and practice. Not only did the ancient world lack the kind of mass communication that allows us to do a quick search for information on other religions with a touch of a screen, but very few people had the chance to travel abroad. As a common peasant, it's likely that Jesus would have stayed in close proximity to the areas surrounding Nazareth and Jerusalem.

However, this doesn't mean that Jesus' teachings necessarily lack similarities to other religious traditions. For instance, several thoughtful books document the similarities between the wisdom traditions rooted in the historical Jesus and the Buddha. And while it's doubtful that Jesus studied "comparative religions" in the same way that a university student might do today, it's fair to suggest that the influence of religious traditions such as Zoroastrianism—which had significantly influenced Judaism in the centuries leading up to Jesus' birth—would've been operative in Jesus' experiences of Judaism.

Yet even more important than these factors is the recognition that the ideology of the Roman Empire—which was ubiquitous in ancient Palestine—functioned like a religion. It's simply impossible to understand the significance of Jesus' life and ministry without recognizing both his awareness of Roman imperial theology and his direct challenges to it.

Throughout the Roman Empire, thousands of monuments, coins, and artworks (not to mention Roman soldiers) reminded subjects of one very important religious point: Caesar was *divi filius*, which means "son of God" in Latin. Make no mistake: Jesus and his followers were martyred because they stood up to Roman imperial theology and offered a very different picture of what God looked like.

Becky Garrison

A. While Jesus was steeped in the study and practices of Judaism, he had a familiarity of the prevailing Greco-Roman culture. Even though he was aware of the Temple practices, there is no evidence to suggest that he ever partook of these rituals. Furthermore, Jesus never proclaimed he was launching a new religion but rather was the fulfillment of the law.

Scriptural References

Deuteronomy 6:4–5; Isaiah 53; Matthew 5:17–20; Mark 1:1, 15; 12:28–34; Luke 2:21–52; 4:18–19; Acts 17

Suggested Additional Sources for Reading

- Amy-Jill Levine, *The Misunderstood Jew: The Church and the Scandal of the Jewish Jesus* (HarperOne, 2007).
- Amy-Jill Levine, Dale Allison, and John Dominic Crossan, *The Historical Jesus in Context* (Princeton Univ. Press, 2006).
- James H. Charlesworth, *The Historical Jesus: An Essential Guide* (Abingdon Press, 2008).
- John Prine, *Jesus: The Missing Years*, audio recording (Oh Boy Records, 1991).
- John Howard Yoder, *The Jewish-Christian Schism Revisited* (Eerdmans, 2003).
- Brad H. Young, *Jesus the Jewish Theologian* (Hendrickson, 1995).
- N. T. Wright, *The Challenge of Jesus* (InterVarsity Press, 1999).
- Glenn Stassen and David P. Gushee, *Kingdom Ethics* (IVP Academic, 2003).
- N. T. Wright, *What St. Paul Really Said* (Eerdmans, 1997).
- Marcus Borg, *Jesus and Buddha: The Parallel Sayings* (Ulysses Press, 1997).
- Thich Nhat Hanh, *Living Buddha, Living Christ* (Riverhead, 1995).
- Amy Jill Levine, *The Misunderstood Jew: The Church and the Scandal of the Jewish Jesus* (HarperOne, 2007).
- E. P. Sanders, *Jesus and Judaism* (Fortress Press, 1985).
- John Dominic Crossan, *God and Empire* (HarperOne, 2007).

Suggested Questions for Further Discussion/Thought

1. Would discovering that Jesus' ministry was influenced by other faiths be comforting or discouraging to you? Why?
2. Think of a time when you encountered another faith. What differences did you notice? What similarities?
3. What does it mean for Christianity that other faiths see Jesus as the Messiah too?
4. How would Jesus respond to the thousands of denominations that call themselves "Christian"?

5. How would Jesus respond to the Islamic understanding of him as a great prophet but not the Son of God?
6. Do you think Jesus wanted to start an entirely new religion?
7. Jarrod claims the Jewishness of Jesus is crucial to understanding the Christian faith. How important is it to you?

Question

43. In John 20:2, it mentions "the other disciple, the one whom Jesus loved." Who is this? Why not name that person? Was it a man or woman? What kind of "love" is the author talking about?

David Lose

Who is...
David Lose

I love almost anything that combines peanut butter and chocolate.

A. Contrary to tradition, odds are that the beloved disciple was not John, son of Zebedee. The beloved disciple was probably a male. He may have been one of Jesus' disciples, but probably not one of the Twelve. He was likely the leader of a group of early Christians expelled from a Jewish synagogue (this was not infrequent in the years after the destruction of the Jerusalem Temple a decade, or more, earlier). This community stood at something of a distance from the more "mainstream" communities focused on the traditions associated with Peter, a tension that bubbles to the surface at several points in the narrative.

In John's gospel, it is the beloved disciple—beloved from *phileo*, Greek for "the love of siblings"—not Peter, who sits close to the Lord at the last supper (John 13:23). While Peter has denied and abandoned his Lord, the beloved disciple stands at the foot of the cross and is commanded to take Jesus' mother as his own (John 19:26–27). Later, the beloved disciple beats Peter in a footrace to the empty tomb, and when he enters he, unlike Peter, instantly believes (John 20:3–8).

Finally, the beloved disciple is the first to recognize Jesus on the beach (John 21:7). He is, at least according to the Fourth Gospel, better liked, faster, and smarter than Peter. So whoever this disciple really was, we know that he was beloved not only by Jesus but especially by his congregation, a Christian community that revered his teaching and tried—successfully—to gain a hearing for his witness to Jesus in the early church.

Who is "the other disciple, the one whom Jesus loved"?

Brandon Gilvin

The character "the disciple whom Jesus loved" is first mentioned in John 13:23, and is mentioned in several other passages (John 19:25–27; 20:1–10; 21:1–14, 20–24). This character is never mentioned in any other gospel. John 19:25–7 implies that the disciple is male, and that he, like Peter, has a special significance and authority for the communities that produced and read John. John 21:24 names the beloved disciple as the author of John.

Likewise, the Greek words used to describe the beloved disciple's relationship with Jesus—*agapao* and *phileo*—connote nothing sexual. Despite occasional suggestions that the beloved disciple was a same-sex lover or even Mary Magdalene, the more likely scenario is that this is an idealized figure, with possible historical antecedent, who was held in high esteem for his role in the spread of the early Jesus movement.

Scriptural References

John 13:23; 19:25–27; 20:1–10; 21.1–14, 20–24

Suggested Additional Source for Reading

• Enter the Bible: http://www.enterthebible.org.

Suggested Questions for Further Discussion/Thought

1. Matthew, Mark, and Luke share a strong "family resemblance," whereas John is distinct at a number of points. As you read John's gospel carefully, what distinct emphases do you notice?
2. There was some discussion among early church leaders about whether or not John should be included as one of the gospels? What do you think?
3. Is the Jesus of John different than the Jesus presented in Matthew, Mark, and Luke? Does this present a challenge or an opportunity for enrichment of your faith? Why?

Question

44. It seems like there are a lot of parallels between the stories of Jesus and the Egyptian mythology character, Horus. Could timelines be wrong somewhere, and could it be that the stories of Horus and Jesus actually are referring to the same person?

Pablo A Jiménez

The idea of a miraculously conceived divine being is not exclusive to the Bible. Several divinities from different pantheons boast extraordinary origins. In ancient Egypt, Horus was the god of the sky and, therefore, the nation's protector. Horus was one of the oldest Egyptian divinities and was considered as Egypt's patron god. Horus was the son of Isis, who conceived him miraculously. In one of his hypostases, or manifestations, Horus was considered a savior.

In Greek mythology, Athena was also born miraculously. Her mother, Metis, was pregnant. Trying to prevent the birth of his daughter, Zeus swallowed Metis. The goddess gave birth to Athena inside Zeus. After complaining of strong headaches, Zeus asked Hephaestus to split open his head. After the procedure, Athena burst out fully armed.

In addition, the biographies of gods or "aretalogies" were common in Greek literature. Therefore it is not strange to find stories about extraordinary men who became gods.

The story of Jesus is different on two crucial points. The first one is the incarnation, or the idea that God became a human being. Given the negative view of the body in Greek culture, the idea of God becoming a man was extraordinary. The second one is monotheism. Romans would have had little trouble with Jesus if he would have been considered just another god, demigod, or divinized hero. However, the church proclamation stressed that there is only one God, in direct opposition to Roman imperial theology.

Mark Van Steenwyk

I had a friend walk away from Christianity because he came to the conclusion that everything in Jesus' story was simply a rip-off from an earlier myth. I remember trying to convince him that Jesus was unique, but in the end, he remained unconvinced. He felt that I had a vested interest in maintaining Jesus' uniqueness and was, therefore, not as reliable as the seemingly "overwhelming" evidence that the gospels were simply rehashing older stories like the myth of Horus.

To be fair, the story of Horus certainly predates Christianity. And it is also true that there are similarities. The cycle of birth, death, and rebirth is found in many mythologies. It is also found in the changing of seasons.

Folks claim, however, that the story of Jesus borrows the following from the story of Horus:[21] Horus was born of a virgin, the only child of the chief god (Osiris). His mother's name was Meri (sounds like Mary, doesn't it?), had twelve disciples, walked on water, cast out demons, was crucified, was resurrected by his father, and is now enthroned in heaven. There are even more similarities claimed.

There are two big problems with drawing too close of a comparison between Jesus and Horus. First, most of the supposed similarities rely on sources that aren't readily available. In other words, the folks who write about this claim to have found largely "hidden" sources that nobody else has access to.

Second, the comparisons are often a stretch. For example, Jesus' mom is named "Mary" but Horus mom is named "Isis-Meri." But "Meri" isn't a name, but rather a title. *Meri* is the Egyptian word for "beloved." Most other connections are also a bit of a stretch.

So while Jesus may have a lot in common with the heroes of other religions, he is unique. Similarities will always exist—after all, humans share a remarkable number of deep spiritual longings. And since Jesus came to fulfill those longings, it makes sense that his story would bear some resemblance to the stories that sprang from such longings.

Suggested Additional Sources for Reading

- "Comparison of the Lives of Horus and Jesus: Coincidence?," http://paganizingfaithofyeshua.netfirms.com/comparsison_horus_jesus_chart.htm.
- Jimmy Dunn, "Horus, the God of Kings," http://www.touregypt.net/featurestories/horus.htm.
- "Isn't the Jesus Story Just a Retelling or 'Copycat' of Earlier Godmen Stories?," http://www.kingdavid8.com/Copycat/Home.html.
- D. M. Murdock, *Christ in Egypt* (Stellar House, 2009).
- Richard A. Gabriel, *Jesus the Egyptian* (iUniverse, 2005).

Suggested Questions for Further Discussion/Thought

1. After considering the sources mentioned previously that compare Horus and Jesus, do you think the similarities are coincidence or more than that?
2. Why do you think there are so many similarities among stories of faith and folklore? Does this affect your thinking about stories in scripture?
3. Do you believe the "Spirit" or essence of Christ may have been expressed in other times and cultures? Why or why not?

21. "Comparison of the Lives of Horus and Jesus: Coincidence?," http://www.pagan izingfaithofyeshua.netfirms.com/comparsison_horus_jesus_chart.htm.

Question

45. Why were books like the infancy gospels of James and Thomas not included in the Bible, especially since they include stories about Jesus' childhood not included in the other gospels?

David Lose

By about the middle of the third century, most Christian communities were reading more or less the same books and these were eventually bound together as the New Testament. Dan Brown aside, there were no councils, no official decrees, and no conspiracies, but the process was as slow as it was simple. Simple, in that the books eventually recognized as the New Testament were those that stood the test of time. (Kind of like we keep listening to the best of the best vintage rock and roll songs—what we call the classics—not all that were released, not even all those that spent a glorious week in the Top 40.) But for this reason, the process was also slow. It took a couple hundred years to winnow through the chaff to get to the wheat.

So the infancy gospels of James and Thomas, like many of the other recently "high profile" gospels (like those of Peter, Thomas, and Judas), weren't included in the Bible largely because people didn't find them all that inspiring. They may have been entertaining, but didn't prove to be edifying.

So while early Christians (both gospels of James and Thomas were probably written around 150 C.E.) may have had an appetite for details of Mary's conception and sustained virginity (James) or delighted in hearing tales of the rather mischievous, if at times cruel, wonder-boy Jesus (Thomas), over time they didn't find these stories all that helpful to their Christian faith and lives. And eventually, they didn't even find them all that interesting, as fewer and fewer people bothered to read or copy them.

Tripp Fuller

The books that made it into the New Testament were those that resonated with the worshiping communities and were understood to be trustworthy in their origin and content. The infancy gospels are not a deep dark secret the church has been hiding but simply unfit for the Bible. When you read them you do not find the Jesus of Matthew, Mark, Luke, and John but imaginative narratives that fill in the gaps from what was in the familiar gospels.

Think of them like the TV series *Smallville*, which depicts the adolescence of Clark Kent (i.e., Superman). *Smallville* is not part of the "official Superman story" but any hardcore Superman fan has thought about what his early years

153

were like. Why? Because they love Superman! But one problem with these documents is that the character of Jesus is not preserved.

For example, in the Thomas' infancy gospel Jesus is depicted as a young boy who can get angry and kill someone with his super powers while Mary and Joseph are stuck doing cover-up. Another issue is the late dating of the documents. One way we know this is by how the stories are clearly directed to a theological issue not present until further into the church's history. For example, the infancy gospel of James spends sixteen of its twenty-four chapters proving the purity of Mary the Mother of Jesus by giving a play by play of her purity from her own birth to her continued virginity after the birth of Jesus.

There is nothing wrong with reading these stories but it is important to remember that, despite their titles, they are not gospels because they do not tell the good news of Jesus' ministry, mission, death, and resurrection.

Pablo A. Jiménez

A. Simply put, the infancy gospels were excluded from the Bible because they are unreliable. These documents were written after the four gospels. They tend to embellish Jesus' story, adding fantastic accounts, just as the infancy gospel of Thomas.

However, the main challenge presented by the noncanonical gospels is theological. They tend to interpret Jesus through Greco-Roman categories. Given that Greek thought had a negative view of the body (in particular) and of matter (in general), most noncanonical gospels present a spiritualized view of Jesus that denies his full humanity. This is the case with the infancy gospel of James.

In theological terms, the noncanonical gospels tend to present a "docetic" view of Jesus. Docetism is the belief that Jesus only "appeared" to be human, for in reality he was a spirit. The term is based in the Greek verb *dokeo*, which means "to appear."

These docetic gospels denied Jesus' death on a cross. He only seemed to die. And of course, if Jesus did not die then he did not rise up from the dead. Instead, they affirmed Jesus' ascension to the heavens, where he truly belonged.

The noncanonical gospels were key to the first heresy faced by the early church: Gnosticism. The Greek word *gnosis* means "science" and "knowledge." Gnostic preachers affirmed that they had a special knowledge passed through generations from Jesus himself. This knowledge was that Jesus was not really a human being but an "emanation" or manifestation of the *logos*, a preexisting divine entity.

In sum, the church rejected most noncanonical gospels because they affirmed a theology that ran counter to the core message of the Christian faith.

Scriptural References

Gospels of James, Thomas, Mary, and Judas (all noncanonical)

Suggested Additional Sources for Reading

- David Lose, *Making Sense of Scripture* (Augsburg Fortress Press, 2009).
- Enter the Bible: http://www.enterthebible.org.

Suggested Questions for Further Discussion/Thought

1. If could only choose five of the New Testament books to read, which five would you choose? Why?
2. Have you read any of the noncanonical gospels discussed previously? Do you feel they should be included as part of scripture? Why or why not?
3. How important to your faith is it that Jesus was a real, fully human being who lived, died, and was resurrected?

46. Jesus forgave people of their sins before he died. How could he do this if he actually had to die in order to save us from sin?

Phil Snider

Who is...
Phil Snider

Despite all my progressive sensibilities, I can't help but love Karl Barth.

For many years, I sat in church quietly wondering why God's forgiveness was based on the idea that awful violence had to be inflicted upon Jesus in order for God to save us from sin. I was never comfortable with this idea, but I feared voicing my questions would make my Christian friends think I was a hell-bound heretic.

It was only when I went to seminary that I learned this wasn't the only way to view Jesus' death, and I'm glad to say I no longer believe Jesus had to die in order to save us from sin.

As it turns out, the idea that Jesus had to die on the cross in order for God to forgive our sins took nearly a thousand years to develop, and numerous theologians have pointed to its problematic implications. Chief among these concerns are questions related to God's power and God's character. In terms of God's power, why is it necessary for God to sacrifice God's Son in order to grant forgiveness? Is there, as Frederiek Depoortere says, "some higher authority or necessity above God with whom God has to comply in doing this"?[22]

In terms of God's character, can't such a belief make God out to be "a *perverse* subject who plays obscene games with humanity and His own Son,"[23] like the narcissistic governess from Patricia Highsmith's *Heroine* who sets the family house on fire in order to be able to prove her devotion to the family by bravely saving the children from the raging flames?

Instead, my Christian faith is grounded in the affirmation that God's love is unconditional, which leads me to believe that God's forgiveness is unconditional as well. All of which means that Jesus' unconditional forgiveness—offered before he died—is one of the things that makes him most Godlike!

---

22. Frederiek Depoortere, *Christ in Postmodern Philosophy* (New York: T & T Clark, 2008), 98.

23. Ibid., quoted from Slavoj Žižek, *The Fragile Absolute* (New York: Verso, 2000), 157.

Amy Reeder Worley

A. I'm a lawyer. My first reaction on reading this particular banned question was to leap from my desk and shout, "Objection! This question assumes facts not in evidence." Yes, I know that is weird. But it's also true. The question as posed assumes that Jesus had to die to "save" people from sin. I don't find much biblical or historical evidence to support this "substitutionary atonement" theory of Jesus' crucifixion and resurrection.

Rather I agree with Marcus Borg and other postmodern theologians who argue that Jesus died *because of* human sin, not in the place of humans who sin. As it relates to the question at hand, my view of the crucifixion means necessarily that forgiveness of sin emanates directly from God, and it existed before, during, and after Jesus' life and resurrection. Like many religious ideas, God's forgiveness operates outside of our limited view of space-time.

So how is it, exactly, that Jesus had the authority to forgive people? Sacred texts throughout the world speak of forgiving our enemies as a sacred and holy act. When Jesus forgave the unclean, criminal, and Gentile he embodied God's preexisting forgiveness of us all, teaching his followers that forgiveness was not limited to the religiously "in" crowd of the day.

In Matthew 9:1–8, Jesus forgives and then heals a paralyzed man. The rabbis accuse Jesus of blasphemy for claiming the authority to forgive sins, an authority they believed was reserved for YHWH. Jesus responds, "Why do you think evil in your hearts? For which is easier, to say, "Your sins are forgiven," or to say, "Stand up and walk"? But so that you may know that the Son of man has authority on earth to forgive sins, Jesus turned to the paralytic and healed him. The crowd was "filled with awe, *and they glorified God, who had given such authority to human beings.*" Here, as throughout the gospels, Jesus reaffirms the message that God's love and forgiveness are available to all of us, all of the time.

Tripp Fuller

A. One could answer the question by saying that Jesus knew he was going to die and rise so he could forgive with the future known and certain or possibly that Jesus' divine identity gave him the ability to forgive sin at will, or one could even suggest that if forgiveness could be given before the cross, then the cross may not have been necessary.

In forgiving sins, Jesus is acting on behalf of God and was one of the reasons Jesus was opposed by the religious leaders, thus forcing one to explain how Jesus' identity is tied to that of God. To understand this, I have found it helpful to see how Paul reimagined the sacrificial system in light of Christ's work.

How could Jesus forgive people of their sins before he died?

Traditionally an act of sacrifice began with the sinner transferring their identity to the animal through an act of consecration. Afterward the animal was killed so that the person was reincorporated into the people of God. Paul reverses the process so that it begins with Christ identifying with us and ends with the consecration, us identifying with that which is sacrificed.

In a sense Paul sees, in Christ, God coming to put an end to sacrifice by turning it upside down and beginning with God's coming to sinner with good news. From this perspective it would make sense that Jesus could forgive sin without having died because God had come in Christ to consecrate the world as God's beloved.

Scriptural References

Matthew 9:2; 18:21; Mark 2:5; Luke 5:20; 7:48; 15:11–32; 23:34

Suggested Additional Sources for Reading

- Any of Marcus Borg's books on Jesus and Christianity
- Rita Nakashima Brock and Rebecca Ann Parker, *Proverbs of Ashes* (Beacon Press, 2002).
- Frederiek Depoortere, *Christ in Postmodern Philosophy* (T & T Clark, 2008).
- Slavoj Žižek, *The Fragile Absolute* (Verso, 2000) and *Did Somebody Say Totalitarianism?* (Verso, 2001).

Suggested Questions for Further Discussion/Thought

1. Do you believe that we have the authority to forgive each other in a religiously relevant sense?
2. Why do you believe Jesus was crucified? How does Jesus' forgiveness of sin before his death affect that belief?
3. Looking at the Bible verses mentioned previously, what types of people do the gospel writers talk about forgiving? Why do you think that is?
4. What import do you give to Jesus' statements of forgiveness from the cross?
5. Do you believe the blood sacrifice of an innocent person is necessary in order for God to forgive sin? Have you ever felt uncomfortable accepting this doctrine? If so, why?

uestion

47. Jesus broke certain biblical laws by healing on the Sabbath, associating with non-Jews, and not keeping all of the kosher laws. So how do we know which rules to follow and which are irrelevant to us today?

R. M. Keelan Downton

The clearest place Jesus addresses the idea of rules is his sermon recorded in Matthew and Luke. His treatment of Torah "law" (I think "instruction" is generally a better translation) is essentially a critique of legalism, but not one that lets us off the hook.

Jesus both frees his listeners from a static prison of rules that are detached from real life situations and also invites them to explore their own intentions more deeply as a way to embody the reign of God. Jesus is not providing a new set of rules (that are more or less difficult to follow depending on how you look at them) but rather advocating a new way of thinking about the rules that focuses on the trajectories they create for communities and the way they support or inhibit relationships between humans and with all creation.

It is important to realize that, though Jesus gets into some arguments over this, he is not the first (or the last) Jewish teacher to approach the Torah this way. Figuring out which instructions given to ancient Hebrews can continue to lead us into wise living today therefore requires being in dialogue with a community about where obedience to such instruction would take the community. It is always a complex process and is made more so by the fact that so many people are part of multiple communities with differing norms.

Following Jesus in this endeavor means starting with the instruction to love God fully and following it with the instruction to love our neighbors with the same love we have for ourselves.

Amy Reeder Worley

The Bible is internally inconsistent, so, as Karen Armstrong points out in *The Case for God*, "our reading is always selective." In fact, it is political. Throughout biblical history, religious teachers like Jesus have interpreted biblical texts through the lens of the political and cultural context of their time.

Jesus was a Jew living in Judea during Roman imperial rule. His world was one of wide-scale oppression, poverty, and disenfranchisement of religious and cultural minorities. His selective reading of Jewish texts offered an interpretation of Jewish law that spoke to the present political and cultural situation in Rome as he experienced it.

Jesus emphasized the "spirit" of Jewish law—liberation from spiritual and political oppression. In healing on the Sabbath, associating with non-Jews, and not keeping kosher, Jesus demonstrated a loving and compassionate Judaism that was less concerned with the edicts of the priesthood and more concerned with the suffering of people. His example teaches that religious legalism should not be used to oppress, exclude, or ignore God's people.

Consistent with Jesus' example, we should be cautious that we don't employ biblical literalism to injure God's people. Unfortunately Christianity, like most other monotheistic religions, has been used to justify slavery and poverty and as an alleged "reason" for natural disasters, disease, and pestilence. If anything, Jesus' message was that such actions are contrary to true faith.

Chris Haw

Who is...
Chris Haw

I live in "America's most dangerous city."

The early church, we are told, saw a great many conversions. But what is most likely is that these early adherents were "God fearers," meaning they were Gentiles that had, previous to Jesus, associated themselves with the Jewish community by enjoying some of their festivals and customs. They already knew Jewish history. The common code of conduct that such persons had to obey was *not* the Mosaic law but only the Noachide covenant: refraining from meat sacrificed to idols, sexual immorality, and so on. The early church apparently used the same criteria, as seen in the book of Acts and Paul's teachings.[24]

24. "In the period prior to the Christ-event, the Jewish view of gentiles who wanted to be associated with Israel was quite clear. Gentiles were perceived as being under the Noahide Law and by obedience to this a gentile became a *Ger Toshav* and was ensured of a portion in the world to come, but remained a gentile. Such obedient gentiles were in some sense associates of Israel, but were clearly distinguished from the *Ger Tzedek* who was regarded as no longer a gentile because he had accepted circumcision and Torah, and was now perceived as being reborn into the household of Israel," in William S. Campbell, *Paul and the Creation of Christian Identity* (London: T & T Clark, 2006), 56. See also, John Howard Yoder, *The Jewish Christian Schism Revisited* (Grand Rapids: Eerdmans, 2003), 56.

But it is particularly provocative to note that the temptation of the early church was not to lean away from Judaism *but to become almost identical to it*. Many in the church thought that potential members should *join the entire story*, not only becoming God fearers, but fully initiated Jews through the Abrahamic ritual of circumcision and concomitant expectation of following all Mosaic laws. But the church rejected that approach and, almost sadly in my opinion, so little is expected of the average Gentile joiner—well, all except "believing in Jesus," which is no easy task.

Later, when Christianity spread into places that had not even heard about Jewish history, the church needed to train people in those stories—otherwise a "conversion" would be too fast, dry, and meaningless, seeing as Jesus can only be seen when backlit by the Passover, exodus, the Prophets, the Temple and king stories, and so on. Once the church needed to labor at explaining these things it began the *catechumenate*, or entry process, of slowly bringing believers into the fold over a (sometimes three-year) long period of time.

In sum, Gentiles enter into the story of God's salvation "through faith" in Jesus—and what that means is quite a blur to me—and are only constrained to follow the Noahide law: refraining from blasphemy, idolatry, adultery, bloodshed, robbery, and eating flesh cut from living animals.[25]

L. Shannon Moore

Who is...
L. Shannon Moore

If I could only hear one song for the rest of my life, it would be "Calling Occupants of Interplanetary Craft" as recorded by the Carpenters.

A. While Jesus did come to bring the good news, heal the sick, and reveal God in a new way, we have to remember that he did not want to throw the proverbial baby out with the bathwater. He grew up with the laws of his ancestors and, for the most part, seemed to keep them. He even said, "Do not think I have come to abolish the law or the prophets" (Matthew 5:17). Clearly, he thought the law was important. So why did he break some of them?

Well, let's take a look at one of the times when he did. In Matthew, Mark, and Luke, religious leaders criticize Jesus' disciples for plucking heads of grain to eat on the Sabbath. Jesus, defending them, references a story about the much-revered Israelite king David who also broke a law when he and his

---

25. See also *b. Aboda Zara* 64b; cf. *b. Sanhedrin* 56a; Dunn 143f.

companions were hungry. In Mark's version he then says, "The [S]abbath was made for humankind, and not humankind for the [S]abbath" (Mark 2:27).

And I think that pretty much sums it up for us. Laws and rules are generally set forth for us to guide us, to protect us, and to lead us in certain directions. The biblical laws protected God's people from eating foods that might make them sick and gave them guidelines for moral behavior. But when we follow laws and rules to the extreme, they can become harmful (see the "Flagellants," the medieval sect who beat themselves and each other as a form of repentance).[26] We should follow the rules until they become destructive, harmful, or irrelevant.

Peter J. Walker

In Mark 2, Jesus responds to questions about picking grain on the Sabbath: "The sabbath was made for humankind, and not humankind for the sabbath" (Mark 2:27). Clearly, Jesus was able to prioritize what was truly important. Can we be trusted to do the same? Whether we can or not, we're already doing it.

Countless books have been written to defend or discount every rule found in scripture; often the most devout people have the hardest time accepting "gray areas." But the God of scripture is a God of gray, and no example proves that point better than Jesus himself.

When Christians were persecuted in Acts 5, a revered Pharisee named Gamaliel cautioned the Sanhedrin, "So in the present case, I tell you, keep away from these men and let them alone; because if this plan or this undertaking is of human origin, it will fail; but if it is of God, you will not be able to overthrow them—in that case you may even be found fighting against God" (Acts 5:38–39).

As the church, we need to make room for God's voice among dissenters, rebels, and radicals. As individual believers, I advocate John Wesley's approach: urging Christians to weigh the voice of God through scripture, tradition, experience, and reason. None of these (not even scripture) is objectively reliable enough to trust alone. And we must honestly search our own motives: *Am I trying to prove a point, feed my ego, satisfy a hidden agenda, or stir division?*

In Matthew 12, Jesus says, "But if you had known what this means, 'I desire mercy and not sacrifice,' you would not have condemned the guiltless" (Matthew 12:7). Choosing how to interpret Biblical laws should never be a matter of condemnation or self-differentiation but of humble striving for wholeness, truth, and wisdom.

---

26. *Encyclopedia Britannica Online*, s.v. "Flagellants," http://www.britannica.com/EBchecked/topic/1373234/flagellants.

Scriptural References

Matthew 5:17–18; 12:1–8; Mark 2:23–28; Luke 6:1–5; Acts 5:17–39

Suggested Additional Sources for Reading

- Karen Armstrong, *The Case for God* (Knopf, 2009).
- Marcus Borg, *Jesus: Uncovering the Life, Teachings, and Relevance of a Religious Revolutionary* (HarperSanFrancisco, 2006).
- Brian D. McLaren, *The Secret Message of Jesus: Uncovering the Truth That Could Change Everything* (Thomas Nelson, 2007).
- A. J. Jacobs, *The Year of Living Biblically: One Man's Humble Quest to Follow the Bible as Literally as Possible* (Simon and Schuster, 2008).
- William S. Campbell, *Paul and the Creation of Christian Identity* (T & T Clark, 2006).
- John Howard Yoder, *The Jewish-Christian Schism Revisited* (Eerdmans, 2003).

Suggested Questions for Further Discussion/Thought

1. What are some other examples of laws or rules that become dangerous when taken to extremes?
2. Does it demonstrate a lack of faith to question biblical laws rather than just following them because we are instructed to?
3. Where is the line between keeping the spirit of Jesus' teaching and theological relativism?
4. Do you think the Bible is a living document, subject to continuous interpretation, or a book that's "plain meaning" should be followed as literally as possible?
5. Did Jesus actually break the law, or was he privy to special insights we can't understand?
6. Jesus said in Matthew 7:12, "In everything do to others as you would have them do to you; for this is the law and the prophets." Can we take him at his word, or was he just trying to make a point?
7. Paul wrote in Galatians 5:14, "For the whole law is summed up in a single commandment, 'You shall love your neighbour as yourself.'" Can it be that simple? What happens if we live that way?

48. Why would God put an unwed teenage mother through the difficulty of pregnancy, childbirth, and trying to explain how she got pregnant?

Joan Ball

Who is...
Joan Ball

I play the bass.

A. Mary was not a victim. She was called into service and faced the challenges that resulted from accepting that calling. Sacrificial service is a recurring theme through both the Old and New Testaments of the Bible. Time and again ordinary men and women are presented with an opportunity to serve in ways that stretch them beyond their capacity to endure without divine assistance, strength, and mercy.

Mary submitted her will and her life to God and persevered when the going got tough. Thus is the life of one for whom songs like "I Surrender All" are more than a heartfelt tune. Applying our best rational thinking to the altogether supernatural and mysterious exchange between Mary and the Father, Son, and Holy Spirit cannot help but raise unanswerable questions.

We humans, particularly educated westerners, do not handle unanswerable questions very well. We like to believe that our science, psychology, sociology, and so on are capable of precisely describing the world, and we are dismissive or skeptical of things that do not fit squarely into this rather arbitrary framework we've created to explain it. Why did God do it this way? I cannot be sure, but I have been motivated and inspired by the example Mary set for modern Christ followers like me.

Brandon Gilvin

A. I would suggest reframing this question in light of a couple of things: Of the four gospels in the Bible, only two (Matthew and Luke) tell the story of Mary's pregnancy. Mark, generally considered to be the earliest of the four gospels, does not mention Mary's pregnancy or any scandal or taboo tied to it nor does Mark suggest that there is anything miraculous about Jesus' birth.

Second, the reference in Matthew to a prophetic text predicting Jesus' birth to a virgin relies on a mistranslation from Hebrew to Greek of Isaiah 7:14. In the Septuagint (the Greek version of the Hebrew Scriptures) the Hebrew word *almah* (young woman) is replaced with *parthenos*, which means "virgin." *Almah* in no way implies anything about the woman's sexual experience. Likewise, the prophecy in Isaiah is not about a future messianic birth, but is about the birth of multiple children, contemporary to the writer, whose names have theological and political meaning.

Furthermore, stories of miraculous birth were common in the first century. Given these facts, I would suggest that the question is not about why God would do such a thing to a young woman. Rather it is a question about why early Christian interpreters and apologists would find it important to make sure that a story of Jesus' miraculous birth was included in the Bible.

Perhaps it was to show that Jesus was as important—if not more important—than Greco-Roman figures such as Hercules, Alexander the Great, or Augustus Caesar. Perhaps it was a way to keep the life of Jesus tied theologically to the Hebrew Scriptures. Perhaps it was a way of covering up an illicit affair that led to Mary's pregnancy. In other words, asking this question about God's intentions allows us to sidestep questions about human motivations surrounding the early Jesus movement.

Sherri Emmons

This one is easy for me, because I simply don't believe in the virgin birth story. The details of Jesus' birth don't really matter to me. What is important is that he lived as an example for all of us, teaching radical hospitality, social justice, care for the poor and alien, and forgiveness.

That said, if I were to take the more traditional view of Jesus' parentage then I guess we have to take the Bible at its word and accept that the pregnancy was an unbelievable honor for a poor young woman. And I would have to believe that God would guide her and protect her through the pregnancy and birth.

Scriptural References

Isaiah 7–9; Lamentations 3:22–33; Matthew 1–2; Luke 1–2

Suggested Additional Sources for Reading

- Watchman Nee, *Sit, Walk, Stand* (Victory Press, 1963).

- Marcus J. Borg and John Dominic Crossan, *The First Christmas: What the Gospels Really Teach about Jesus's Birth* (HarperOne, 2009).
- Marguerite Rigoglioso, *The Cult of Divine Birth in Ancient Greece* (Palgrave Macmillan, 2009).
- J. Gresham Machen, *The Virgin Birth of Christ* (Harper & Brothers, 1930).
- Roger Underwood, "The Virgin Birth: Why I Believe," *DisciplesWorld*, December 2003, 3–4.
- Jimmy R. Watson, "The Virgin Birth: Does It Matter?," *DisciplesWorld*, December 2003, 3, 5.

Suggested Questions for Further Discussion/Thought

1. Does it matter to your faith if Mary was a virgin? Why or why not?
2. What does it tell us about our contemporary culture's understanding of sex and sexuality that this portion of the story of Jesus remains so important to so many?
3. If Jesus was actually the byproduct of human conception—perhaps even of two unwed people—does this compromise his divinity or his ministry? And what might it say about the sanctity of marriage?

49. Why did Jesus heal some people by touching them, some when they touched him, and others without even meeting them? And then why use mud to cure a man from blindness? Did he really need this?

Brandon Gilvin

Jesus' primary message was of the kingdom of God—an eschato-logical vision of the world-made-right. As John Dominic Crossan has said, the kingdom of God was a vision of the world ruled as if God ruled, not Caesar; peace, not war; and wholeness, not brokenness.

When the gospel writers described Jesus' healing ministry, their writings encapsulated this vision of the kingdom. Healing was not a super power nor was it just a recording of the restoration of one's physicality. These are stories of Jesus' ministry, a ministry of bringing wholeness (of all kinds) to a broken world. To ask about Jesus' technique is to miss the point: We as disciples who follow Jesus are called to bring wholeness and healing to a broken, hurting world—one person at a time, no matter their ailment.

Joan Ball

For me, these questions come together into a single one: Why didn't Jesus do things in a more linear, predictable way? It certainly would seem to make more sense to our western, rational minds if Jesus had developed a highly efficient plan of action for healing and had applied it consistently across his ministry. That kind of repetition would allow us to understand Jesus' motivations and maybe even to predict his next move—like watching him work his miracles on a supernatural assembly line.

But Jesus' ministry was more custom artisan than mass production. In the same way I would never ask a fine artist why he or she does not use paint by numbers, I would not expect Jesus Christ to fulfill the will of the Father in a way that I could easily predict or comprehend.

Scriptural References

Matthew 13:44–52

Why did Jesus heal some people by touching them?

Suggested Additional Sources for Reading

- Leonard Sweet, *So Beautiful* (David C. Cook, 2009).
- Makoto Fujimura, *River Grace* (Polema Press, 2007).
- Esther de Waal, *Lost in Wonder* (Liturgical Press, 2003).
- John Dominic Crossan, *God and Empire* (HarperOne, 2007).

Suggested Questions for Further Discussion/Thought

1. Do you think there is a single purpose or message behind Jesus' healing miracles, or was he just responding to the needs in front of him?
2. What does it say about people who Jesus didn't heal? What does it say about the suffering in the world today?
3. Why do you think suffering exists at all? Does it serve a purpose?

50. Did Jesus have a clue that people would call him Messiah or God Incarnate? Would he have tolerated these labels?

José F. Morales Jr.

Who is...
José F. Morales Jr.

I play a mean game of ping pong.

A. Would he have tolerated these labels? Messiah? I think yes. God Incarnate? I'm not sure.

From the beginning up until the early 1900s, the church saw Jesus' proximity to divinity as a given. The Apostles Creed states, "I believe . . . in Jesus Christ, His only Son, our Lord: Who was conceived by the Holy Ghost."

Since the scientific age, much of the church's traditional Christology has been viewed as suspect or superstitious. Unfortunately for traditionalists, you can just say, "It's in the Bible!" When the early church compiled the Bible, it included multiple (at times conflicting) theologies about Jesus within its pages. Let's take the gospels for example:

- Mark speaks of the God *of* Jesus. Jesus makes a clear distinction between himself and God (Mark 10:18).
- Matthew and Luke portray God *in or through* Jesus. For example, Jesus is born of the Holy Spirit in Luke and is worshipped in Matthew, something Mark's Jesus probably wouldn't allow (Luke 1:35; Matthew 28:17).
- John is all about God *as* Jesus. Jesus is the Word who "was God" and who "became flesh" (John 1:1, 14).

So with all these divergent views, was there any common ground among the first believers? I think there are two:

- Jesus was the Messiah, the anointed one ("Christ"). This belief is upheld in most of the New Testament, though it should be noted that "messiah" didn't necessarily mean "God" (Isaiah 45:1, in which the Persian King Cyrus is called "messiah"). Jesus accepts this title in the gospels.
- Martin Marty succinctly summarizes the second common point about Jesus in the New Testament: "[T]he human Jesus is the exalted

Lord."[27] Jesus as "Lord" allows for various understandings: same nature as God or not quite God but above mere human.

Where do I fall? Like the disciples in Matthew 28 and the elders in Revelation 5, I pray to Jesus (the Trinity helps me to stay monotheistic). So I gladly sing one of the earliest hymns of the church, which Paul quotes in Philippians 2: "Christ Jesus . . . in the form of God" (vv. 5–6). Yet I want to take Mark seriously and not just John, so I agree with N. T. Wright that the earthly Jesus did not know he was God in the same way he knew he was Jewish. But he had a hunch about his divine vocation.[28]

Christian Piatt

Who is...
Christian Piatt

I met my wife on a blind date.

A big deal is made in the Old Testament about the name of God being unmentionable. While some think of this as indicating the holiness of the Almighty, I tend to think of it as an act of utter futility. How, after all, could such a limiting tool as human language ever accurately describe the essence of the ultimate source of all life?

Jesus, however, had no such hang-ups about his understanding of God. He even went as far as calling God *Abba* (best translated as "daddy" in English) and made clear that he had a special relationship with God. Over and again, he says that he is the one who points to God, the "way" to God and is sent by God to the world. There are a number of definitions of what a messiah is, all of which Jesus fulfills. He embraces the identity of savior, liberator, and one for whom so many have waited.

As for being called God Incarnate, it seems to me that he would be less pleased with such an identity. In many instances, particularly in John (6:39; 8:29; 16:5) Jesus refers to the one who sent him, referring to God. So Jesus distinguishes between himself and God, and so it would seem he would expect us to think of him likewise.

In the end, though, Jesus is way less concerned with labels than he is with getting down to the business of real ministry. Sure, there are all of the "I am"

27. Martin Marty, *The Christian World: A Global History* (New York: Modern Library, 2007).

28. N. T. Wright, *The Challenge of Jesus: Rediscovering Who Jesus Was and Is* (Downers Grove, IL: InterVarsity Press, 1999).

statements also found in John but given that this focus is really only emphasized in John, this may tell us more about the author of that gospel and what
he wanted to communicate to readers rather than revealing what Jesus wanted
people to call him.

I think the passage found in Mark 8:27–33 where Jesus asks his disciples
who they say he is actually is more telling than any of the "I am" claims of
John. Hardly trying to be coy or mysterious, Jesus understands the human
psyche enough to realize we'll see him how we choose to see him, no matter
who or what he *actually* is. And ultimately, we humans are left to carry on the
mantle Jesus first took up, acting as a mirror, reflecting to a broken, hurting
world the wholeness, peace, healing, and hope we claim to have found in our
relationship with Jesus, the Christ.

Scriptural References

Matthew 28:17–20; Mark 8:27–33; 10:18; Luke 1:26–38; John 1:1–18;
    Philippians 2:5–11; Revelation 4—5

Suggested Additional Sources for Reading

- Marcus J. Borg and N. T. Wright, *The Meaning of Jesus: Two Visions* (HarperOne, 2007).
- Paula Fredriksen, *From Jesus to Christ: The Origins of the New Testament Images of Jesus* (Yale Univ. Press, 2000).
- Stanley J. Grenz, "The Fellowship of Jesus the Christ with God," in *Theology for the Community of God* (Eerdmans, 2000).
- Martin Marty, "The Jewish Beginnings," in *The Christian World: A Global History* (Modern Library, 2008).
- Geza Vermes, *The Changing Faces of Jesus* (Viking Compass, 2001).
- Garry Wills, *What Jesus Meant* (Viking, 2006).
- Garry Wills, *What the Gospels Meant* (Viking, 2008).
- N. T. Wright, *The Challenge of Jesus: Rediscovering Who Jesus Was and Is* (IVP, 2011).

Suggested Questions for Further Discussion/Thought

1. How do you understand the biblical phrases "Jesus is Lord" and "Lord Jesus"?
2. Which portrait of Jesus is most meaningful to you, Mark's or John's?
3. How do you speak of God in relation to Jesus: God of Jesus, God in or through Jesus, or God as Jesus?

Contributors List, Biographies, and Suggested Resources

Contributor: Amy Reeder Worley

Professional title: lawyer

Personal blog: http://conversationsaboutrealandsurreal.blogspot.com

Bio: I am a wife, mother, lawyer, writer, contrarian, and Southern progressive. I am also a spiritual seeker, despite my repeated attempts to give that up for Lent. I grew up in a conservative, evangelical Church of God where I became deeply afraid of, though not in love with, God. After a half-hearted attempt to work out the problems in our relationship, we broke up, God and me.

After some time apart, I decided that God and I should try again, tabula rasa. And so I've spent the past fifteen years engrossed in the self-study of religion, spirituality, and philosophy. I tried being a Buddhist once. I sucked at it.

I currently practice law, mother, and work on my novel in Raleigh, North Carolina. I ended up a Presbyterian. No, it wasn't preordained.

Recommended Books, Web Sites, Blogs, and Other Resources for People to Explore

Karen Armstrong, *A History of God: The 4,000 Year Quest of Judaism, Christian and Islam* (Ballantine, 1994).

Sue Monk Kidd, *The Dance of the Dissident Daughter* (HarperSanFrancisco, 1996).

Thomas Merton, *New Seeds of Contemplation* (New Directions, 1961).

Dalai Lama, *The Universe in a Single Atom: The Convergence of Science and Spirituality* (Morgan Road, 2005).

Paul Knitter, *Without Buddha I Could Not Be a Christian* (Oneworld, 2009).

Thich Nhat Hanh, *Living Buddha, Living Christ* (Riverhead, 1995).

Henry Nouwen, *The Return of the Prodigal Son* (Continuum, 1995).

Marcus Borg, *Meeting Jesus Again for the First Time* (HarperSanFrancisco, 1994).

Anything by Anne Lamott

Favorite Quotes

The Kingdom of God is within you.

—Jesus

Whatever you are, be a good one.

—Abraham Lincoln

To be nobody but yourself in a world which is doing its best day and night to make you like everybody else means to fight the hardest battle which any human being can fight and never stop fighting.

—E. E. Cummings

A lie cannot live.

—Martin Luther King Jr.

I do not at all understand the mystery of grace—only that it meets us where we are but does not leave us where it found us.

—Anne Lamott

Watch your thoughts; they become words.
Watch your words; they become actions.
Watch your actions; they become habits.
Watch your habits; they become character.
Watch your character; for it becomes your destiny.

—Upanishads

Five Things People Can Do Today in Their Own Community to Help Make the World a Better Place

1. Be present. Notice people around you, the ones outside of your head. See their suffering. It is an illusion to think that their pain is not also your pain.
2. Do something. Every community has tremendous local need. Volunteer your time to help. If you don't know what to do, call your local paper ask to speak with the person who writes the "community section." Ask them what volunteer opportunities are available.
3. Tell the truth, loudly. You cannot change the world if you don't tell the truth about the nature of it. Loudly doesn't mean rudely. It means with feeling. The only thing that kills a lie is the truth.
4. Give money to charities that do good work. It doesn't matter how much, only that it should cause you to have to sacrifice something.
5. Repeat number 1.

Contributor: Becky Garrison

Professional title: religious satirist
Personal Web site: http://www.beckygarrison.com
Bio: My books include *Jesus Died for This?* (Zondervan, 2010), *The New Atheist Crusaders and Their Unholy Grail* (Thomas Nelson, 2007), *Rising from the Ashes: Rethinking Church* (Seabury Books, 2007), and *Red and Blue God, Black and Blue Church* (Jossey-Bass, 2006).

Recommended Books, Web Sites, Blogs, and Other Resources for People to Explore

Killing the Buddha: http://www.killingthebuddha.com.
Soujourners: http://www.sojo.net.
Religion Dispatches magazine: http://www.religiondispatches.org.
Proost: http://www.proost.co.uk.
The High Calling: http://www.thehighcalling.org.
Nailin' It to the Church: http://www.nailinittothechurch.com.
The Lone Star Iconoclast: http://lonestaricon.com.
Harvey Cox, *The Future of Faith* (HarperOne, 2009).
Jeff Sharlet, *The Family* (Harper Perennial, 2009).
Thomas Cathcart and Daniel Klein, *Heidegger and a Hippo Walk Through Those Pearly Gates* (Penguin, 2010).
N. T. Wright, *Surprised by Hope* (HarperOne, 2008).
Phyllis Tickle, *The Words of Jesus: A Gospel of the Sayings of Our Lord with Reflections by Phyllis Tickle* (Jossey-Bass, 2008).
Jonathan Swift, *The Writings of Jonathan Swift* (W. W. Norton and Company, 2009).
Henri J. M. Nouwen, ed. Michael Ford, *The Dance of Life: Weaving Sorrows and Blessings into One Joyful Step* (Ave Maria Press, 2005).

Favorite Quotes

Every day *people* are straying away from the church and going back to *God*

—Lenny Bruce

Always look on the bright side of life.

—*Life of Brian*

175

Five Things People Can Do Today in Their Own Community to Help Make the World a Better Place

1. For one day, say thank you to every person who helps you that day: from the bus driver to the supermarket checkout girl to the surly person at the DMV. Once you get though that day, try it again the next day. Eventually it will become second nature.
2. Pay it forward by making a small loan to http://www.kiva.org. When the recipient pays it back, then pay it forward by making a loan to another person in need.
3. Reduce your dependency on processed commercialized food manufactured by multinational corporations by visiting local greenmarkets, participating in the slow food movement, and other ways to develop a diet that is healthier both for you and the planet.
4. Recalculate your carbon footprint in light of the ongoing economic and environmental crises to see how you can reduce travel (e.g., multitask by making longer trips to one area instead of repeated trips; cut down on conference hopping by using Skype, webcasting and other online tools to communicate; and explore carpooling and other sustainable modes of travel).
5. Simplify your life: Reduce your consumption by seeing what you truly need versus what our consumerist culture has tried to sell to you. Make a conscious effort to purchase items that are fair trade, especially those organizations where you know you're helping a woman achieve self-sufficiency instead of contributing to a sweatshop economy.

Contributor: Brandon Gilvin

Professional title: associate director, Week of Compassion—the Relief, Refugee, and Development Ministry of the CC (DOC); and ordained minister

Personal blog: http://www.everydayheresy.wordpress.com

Bio: I am a writer, minister, diasporic Appalachian, theological progressive, and traveler.

Recommended Books, Web Sites, Blogs, and Other Resources for People to Explore

Anything by Amy-Jill Levine

A. J. Jacobs, *The Year of Living Biblically* (Simon and Schuster, 2008).

WTF? (Where's the Faith?) series from Chalice Press.

Favorite Quotes

That is God. A shout in the street.

—James Joyce

I hear leaders quit their lying.
I hear babies quit their crying.
I hear soldiers quit their dying, one and all.
I hear them all.

—Old Crow Medicine Show

Five Things People Can Do Today in Their Own Community to Help Make the World a Better Place

1. Vote.
2. Read a book that takes you out of your comfort zone.
3. Read fiction.
4. Eat local, sustainable food—as often as you can.
5. Find out something about a different culture.

Contributor: Chris Haw

Professional title: adjunct professor of religious studies, Cabrini College; carpenter; and potter

Personal blog: http://chrishaw.blogspot.com

Bio: Chris Haw is an aspiring potter, carpenter, painter, and theologian. Haw and his wife, Cassie, are members of Camden Houses, a multihouse community in Camden, New Jersey. He grew up Catholic, spent many years growing and serving at Willow Creek Community Church outside of Chicago, and a few months studying ecology and theology while living in Belize.

Besides being a mostly full-time carpenter, Haw now enjoys periodically teaching at various congregations, conferences, and classes, as well as hosting with his community small conferences on "the new monasticism."

A graduate of Eastern University with degrees in sociology and theology, Haw did his graduate work in theology at Villanova University and now teaches at Cabrini College.

He coauthored the book *Jesus for President* with Shane Claiborne, has been interviewed in *Christianity Today* and *Sojourners*, and featured in the DVD series *Another World Is Possible* and the documentary *The Ordinary Radicals*.

177

Recommended Books, Web Sites, Blogs, and Other Resources for People to Explore

Movies

Mark Achbar and Jennifer Abbot, directors, *The Corporation* (Big Picture Media, 2003).
Eugene Jarecki, director, *Why We Fight* (BBC Storyville, Canadian Broadcasting, 2005).
Roland Joffé, director, *The Mission* (Warner Bros., 1986).
. . . oh, and many others.

Books

Depends on who I am talking to.

Favorite Quotes

Probably the most urgent question now faced by people who would adhere to the Bible is this: What sort of economy would be responsible to the holiness of life? What, for Christians, would be the economy, the practices and the restraints, of "right livelihood"? I do not believe that organized Christianity now has any idea. I think its idea of a Christian economy is no more or less than the industrial economy—which is an economy firmly founded upon the seven deadly sins and the breaking of all ten of the Ten Commandments.
———Wendell Berry, *Sex, Economy, Freedom, and Community*

"By all the working and orthodox standards of sanity, capitalism is insane. I should not say to Mr. Rockefeller, 'I am a rebel.' I should say 'I am a respectable man: and you are not.'"
—G. K. Chesterton, *Utopia of Usurers*

Five Things People Can Do Today in Their Own Community to Help Make the World a Better Place

1. Grow your own food.
2. Know your neighbors and their needs.
3. Bike.
4. Reduce waste in all its forms and promote greener technologies.
5. Speak straight.

Contributor: Christian Piatt

Professional title: author, editor, and public speaker
  Personal Web sites, e-mail, blog, podcast:
  Web site: http://www.christianpiatt.com
  Podcast: http://christianpiatt.podbean.com
  Blog: http://www.christianpiatt.wordpress.com
  Bio: Christian Piatt is the author of *Lost: A Search for Meaning* (Chalice Press, 2006) and *MySpace to Sacred Space: God for a New Generation* (Chalice Press, 2007), which he coauthored with his wife, Amy Piatt. He coauthored Chalice Press' Lenten Meditation booklet for 2008.

Piatt is an editor for *PULP*, an independent alt-monthly publication for southern Colorado, and he is series cocreator and coeditor of the new *WTF? (Where's the Faith?)* book series for Chalice Press. He is also creator and editor of the *Banned Questions* series.

Christian Piatt speaks, preaches, and facilitates workshops nationally on congregational transformation, young adult spirituality, church and technology, faith and culture, and postmodern spirituality. He consults with religious and educational institutions on communications, social media, and public relations. He is a musician, spoken word artist, and cofounder of Milagro Christian Church in Pueblo, Colorado.

Recommended Books, Web Sites, Blogs, and Other Resources for People to Explore

Taizé: http://www.taize.fr/en—Web site dedicated to the monastic community in Taizé, France.
Cool People Care: http://www.coolpeoplecare.org—Web site that helps people make simple changes in their lives for a better world.
A. J. Jacobs, *The Year of Living Biblically: One Man's Humble Quest to Follow the Bible as Literally as Possible* (Simon and Schuster, 2008).
Christopher Moore, *Lamb: The Gospel According to Biff, Christ's Childhood Pal* (Harper, 2003).

Favorite Quotes

Be the change you want to see in the world.

—Mahatma Gandhi

If there is a problem and there is something you can do about it, don't worry about it; if there is a problem and there is nothing you can do about it, don't worry about it.

—Buddhist proverb

179

Truly, I say to you, as you did it to one of the least of these my brothers, you did it to me.

—Matthew 25:40

Five Things People Can Do Today in Their Own Community to Help Make the World a Better Place

1. Listen more; talk less.
2. Care daily for your mind, body, and spirit. An imbalanced schedule leads to an imbalanced life.
3. Give more than you think you can afford, and accept more than you think you deserve.
4. Know where the things you buy come from. One of your most powerful tools is in your wallet.
5. Pray for wisdom, peace, clarity, and courage, but do not hold God accountable for your personal expectations.

Contributor: David J. Lose

Professional title: Marbury E. Anderson Associate Professor of Biblical Preaching at Luther Seminary, St. Paul, Minnesota.

Personal Web site(s), e-mail, blog, podcast, etc.: http://www.workingpreacher.org; Sermon Brainwave (podcast), found at http://www.workingpreacher.org; Bible Roundtable (podcast, forthcoming this spring), found at http://www.enterthebible.org

Bio: David J. Lose holds The Marbury E. Anderson Chair in Biblical Preaching at Luther Seminary, where he also serves as the director of the Center for Biblical Preaching. He is the author of *Making Sense of Scripture* (2009), *Confessing Jesus Christ: Preaching in a Postmodern World* (2003), and *Making Sense of the Christian Story* (September 2010). He speaks widely in the United States and abroad on preaching, Christian faith in a postmodern world, and biblical interpretation.

Recommended Books, Web Sites, Blogs, and Other Resources for People to Explore

David J. Lose, *Making Sense of Scripture: Big Questions about the Book of Faith* (Augsburg Fortress Press, 2009).
Enter the Bible: http://www.enterthebible.org.
Working Preacher: http://www.workingpreacher.org.

Favorite Quote

Be the change you want to see in the world.

—Mahatma Gandhi

Five Things People Can Do Today in Their Own Community to Help Make the World a Better Place

1. Pray for peace, for justice, for equality, for people you know who are hurting or in need, for people you don't know who are hurting or in need, for someone you don't like, for leaders in the world that they may discern what is right and have the courage to do it.
2. Listen almost every day; you will run into someone who needs you to listen—not to agree or disagree, not to correct or make suggestions, but just to listen. Do that.
3. Reach out almost every day; you will come across someone who is discouraged, down, afraid, or sad. When you find that person, say something encouraging, hopeful, and uplifting.
4. Participate. Whatever we can accomplish alone, together we can accomplish even more. Sometime in the next week, ask members of a group you're part of—a church group, a political group, a book club, whatever—what they're doing to make a difference in the world, and join them in doing it.
5. Share. Find a group or cause that you care about and budget what you can give them each month of your time, your talent, and your money. And then do it.

Contributor: Jarrod McKenna

Professional title: sergeant

Personal Web sites, e-mail, blog, podcast: http://paceebene.org/user/8; http://paceebene.org/blog/jarrod-mckenna; https://suwa.org.au/epyc

Bio: Jarrod McKenna is a failed artist, hack philosopher, recovering achiever, doubting evangelist, larrikin seditionist, one-day-wannabe permaculturalist, lapsed vegetarian, who's now happy to glean his daily bread from dumpsters (but secretly longs for the fleshpots of burgers from evil, big corporations). He spends his time as a nonviolence trainer for activists, students, and anybody else that will listen and sharing the gospel of a nonviolent Messiah (hopefully in more than just words!). He is a cofounder of the Peace Tree Community, serving with the marginalized in one of the poorest areas in his city; heads up Together for Humanity in Western Australia, an interfaith youth initiative serving together for the common good; and is the founder and creative director of Empowering Peacemakers in Your Community (EPYC), for which he has received an Australian Peace Award for his work in empowering a generation of "eco-evangelists and peace prophets," which almost makes him sound respectable . . . almost.

Recommended Books, Web Sites, Blogs, and Other Resources for People to Explore

Pace e Bene: http://paceebene.org/user/8.

Personal blog: http://paceebene.org/blog/jarrod-mckenna.

Scripture Union Western Australia Web site, "Empowering Peacemakers in Your Community," https://suwa.org.au/epyc.

Dave Andrews, *Plan Be* (available at http://www.daveandrews.com.au/pb.html).

Paul Dekar, *Community of the Transfiguration: The Journey of a New Monastic Community* (Lutterworth Press, 2008).

Lee Camp, *Mere Discipleship* (Brazos Press, 2003).

Favorite Quotes

For the earth will be filled with the knowledge of the glory of YHWH, as the waters cover the sea.

—Habakkuk 2:14

You know what the good news is? It's the end of the bad news.

—Adi Leason (Kiwi Ploughshares activist)

The Christian alternative to war is worship.

—Stanley Hauerwas

The future is here. It's just not widely distributed yet.

—William Gibson

It is my firm opinion that [the West] today represents not the spirit of God or Christianity but the spirit of Satan. And Satan's successes are the greatest, when he appears with the name of God on his lips. [The West] today is only nominally Christian. In reality, it is worshipping Mammon. 'It's easier for a camel to pass through the eye of a needle that for a rich man to enter the Kingdom of Heaven.' Thus really spoke Jesus Christ. [Today] His so-called followers measure their moral progress by their material possessions.

—Gandhi

The *poor* tells us who we are, The *prophets* tell us who we could be,
So we *hide the poor*, And *kill the prophets*

—Phil Berrigan

What costs are we willing to undergo? You can't be a Christian, if you're not willing to pick up your cross. And, in the end, be crucified on it. That's the bottom line. The rest of it just sounding brass and tinkling symbols. [the question is] How deep is your love?

—Cornel West

I'd rather go to hell with Jesus than heaven without him.

—Me

Five Things People Can Do Today in Their Own Community to Help Make the World a Better Place

1. Meditate daily on the life, teachings, crucifixion, and resurrection of our Lord. This is something Martin Luther King Jr. had everyone in the civil-rights movement commit to and it's having a powerful effect in my life.
2. Every time you pray, let the Lord's Prayer be a part of it. Let the wonder of "on Earth as it is in heaven" infuse this good news into your psyche until it appears in your dreams. And then let God's dream for creation appear in your waking life.
3. Seek to memorize the Sermon on the Mount. I'm not there yet but this disciple of memorizing scripture finds it very helpful, and it's an amazing grace when the Holy Spirit brings the verses to memory while you are working (start with the Beatitudes).
4. Find two or three people who are willing to hold you accountable to acting on a new imagination of grace. Choose small experiments (e.g., become aware of God's presence in those who are excluded at school or at work and seek to include them) and share it with these two sister or brothers as you move deeper into the grace of discipleship
5. Spend time daily in silence just waiting on the visitation of the presence of God. My experience has been that from this silent surrender I'm able to more fully open to the Triune God's transformation in my life. It's not easy. I often find it hard. But life takes on colors that slowly replace what was black and white. Both the pain and the beauty that were dull become vibrant and can pass through us in prayer. Our love for God and the wonder of God's grace can start to seep out of our wounds into a love for all creation, even our enemies. From this silence let worship well up and over into every part of life.

Contributor: Joan Ball

Professional title: author of *Flirting with Faith: My Spiritual Journey from Atheism to a Faith-Filled Life*

Personal Web site: http://www.flirtingwithfaith.com

Bio: Joan Ball is a professor of communication and marketing and author. A seeker-turned-skeptic who was raised without a prescribed notion of God, she experienced a dramatic and unlikely conversion to Christianity at age thirty-seven. A prolific blogger at Beliefnet.com, her posts reflect an insider/outsider perspective on living a faith that both delights and confounds her. She lives with her husband, Martin, and their eleven-year-old son, Ian, in a northwestern suburb of New York City. Their son Andrew (twenty years old) and daughter Kelsey (nineteen years old) are undergraduates.

Recommended Books, Web Sites, Blogs, and Other Resources for People to Explore

Watchman Nee, *Sit, Walk, Stand* (Victory Press, 1963).
Charles Swindoll, *Grace Awakening* (Word, 1990).
Esther de Waal, *Living with Contradiction* (Harper & Row, 1989).
Thomas Merton, *No Man Is an Island* (Harcourt, Brace, 1955).

Five Things People Can Do Today in Their Own Community to Help Make the World a Better Place

1. Be kind.
2. Learn to be less selfish.
3. Find out what other people need most and give it to them, even if it means giving up something that is important to you.
4. Create something beautiful and share it.
5. Help kids.

Contributor: José F. Morales Jr.

Personal Web site, e-mails: DJ Rhema: http://www.myspace.com/rhemapresents josefrancisco; rhemalogix@yahoo.com; rhemalogix.josefrancisco@gmail.com

Bio: José F. Morales Jr. was born in Puerto Rico in 1978. As a missionary's kid and pastor's kid, he has lived in Venezuela, Ohio, and Chicago. His parents, until recently, served as pastors of a Hispanic Pentecostal congregation in Chicago's economically deprived South Side. He has four sisters, one of which is his twin.

José now resides in Denver, Colorado, currently serving as the transitional regional minister of the Central Rocky Mountain region of the Christian Church (Disciples of Christ).

Prior to this, he served as the associate pastor at Iglesia del Pueblo-Hope Center (IDP) in Hammond, Indiana. IDP is prominently a Hispanic disciples congregation, though it is evolving into a multicultural gathering. He also helped found that congregation's social agency, Hope Center of Northwest Indiana, Inc., and served as its executive director for the first three years. During the last two years at IDP, he served as the Clergy Caucus chair of the Northwest Indiana Federation, an interfaith community organizing network of churches and mosques that addresses issues of justice in the northwest Indiana region in order to effect positive public policy and economic development.

José went to Judson College (affiliated with the American Baptist Convention) in Elgin, Illinois (near Chicago) where he earned a bachelor's degree in communications and biblical studies. In 2005, he graduated from McCormick Theological Seminary (affiliated with the Presbyterian Church USA) in Chicago with a master of divinity. He still maintains strong ties with McCormick, where he currently is on the board of trustees and has served as adjunct professor. He plans on pursuing a Ph.D.

José is a frequent keynote speaker and preacher and a freelance writer. Some of his writings have appeared in *Sojourners* and *DisciplesWorld* magazine. He plays a mean game of ping-pong, is a fan of the Chicago White Sox, and loves urban art and techno and hip-hop music. He is a club DJ part time.

Recommended Books, Web Sites, Blogs, and Other Resources for People to Explore

Theological Texts That Have Shaped (or Are Shaping) Me

Virgilio Elizondo, *Galilean Journey: The Mexican-American Promise* (Orbis, 1983).
Dietrich Bonhoeffer, *The Cost of Discipleship* (SCM Press, 1948).
Stanley Grenz, *Theological for the Community of God* (Broadman and Holman, 1994).
Steven J. Land, *Pentecostal Spirituality: A Passion for the Kingdom* (Sheffield Academic Press, 1993).
Peter J. Gomes, *The Good Book: Reading the Bible with Mind and Heart* (W. Morrow, 1996).
Henri Nouwen, *In the Name of Jesus* (Crossroad, 1989).

Fiction and Creative Nonfiction That Have Shaped (or are Shaping) Me

Chaim Potok, *The Chosen* (Ballantine, 1982).
Sherman Alexie, *Indian Killer* (Atlantic Monthly Press, 1996).

Jhumpa Lahari, *The Namesake* (Houghton Mifflin, 2003).
Chinua Achebe, *Things Fall Apart* (Heinemann, 1958).
Esmeralda Santiago, *When I Was Puerto Rican* (Addison Wesley, 1993).
Malcolm X, *The Autobiography of Malcolm X* (Grove Press, 1965).

Favorite Quotes

I have come that they might have life, and that they might have it more abundantly.

—Jesus of Nazareth

Injustice anywhere is a threat to justice everywhere.

—Martin Luther King Jr.

God is of no importance, unless He is of supreme importance.

—Rabbi Abraham Joshua Heschel

Hope has two beautiful daughters. Their names are anger and courage: anger at the way things are and courage to see that they do not remain the way they are.

—Saint Augustine

Five Things People Can Do Today in Their Own Community to Help Make the World a Better Place

1. To Americans: Become aware of our privilege and our abuse of that privilege in the world; sacrifice comfort.
2. To my people of color: The race struggle is not over just because you got a house in the suburbs; and to whites: Your guilt is not getting us anywhere; repent and reconcile.
3. To consumers: Refuse to accept society's proclamation that we are what we have; embrace simplicity.
4. To church people: Be intentional about your relationship with God and the radical things that that relationship calls for; practice the disciplines.
5. To so-called straight people: If Jesus were here today, he would chill with "the gays"; so I encourage you to chill with Jesus for once; stand in solidarity.

Contributor: R. M. Keelan Downton

Professional title: research professor of theology in the Micah Institute at New York Theological Seminary Communications and public relations specialist for the Woodstock Theological Center at Georgetown University

Personal blog: http://keelandownton.blogspot.com

Bio: Dr. R. M. Keelan Downton is an ongoing participant in the emerging church conversation through the lens of Wesleyan, Anabaptist, and Pentecostal theological traditions with research interests in narrative theology, ecumenism, and peace studies. Downton is author of *Authority in the Church: An Ecumenical Reflection on Hermeneutic Boundaries and Their Implications for Inter-Church Relations* (2006).

Recommended Books, Web Sites, Blogs, and Other Resources for People to Explore

David Louis Edelman, *Jump 225 Trilogy* (Pyr, 2006–2010).
Marge Piercy, *Woman on the Edge of Time* (Knopf, 1976).
Murray Jardine, *The Making and Unmaking of Technological Society* (Brazos Press, 2004).

Favorite Quotes

Driven by the forces of love, the fragments of the world are seeking each other, so that the world may come into being
—Pierre Teilhard de Chardin

The question of bread for myself is a material question, but the question of bread for my neighbors, for everybody, is a spiritual and religious question
—Nicolas Berdyaev

Everything begins with a prophet and ends with a policeman.
—Brendan McCauley

All discourses on exclusion, discrimination, racism, etc. will remain superficial as long as they don't address the religious foundations of the problems that besiege our society.
—Rene Girard, *I See Satan Fall Like Lightning*

Perhaps some people like to go to meetings after a hard day's work and try to focus discussion on the issue, to haggle over the language of a resolution, or gather signatures for a petition, or call long lists of strangers on the telephone. But most people would rather watch television, read poetry, or make love.

—Iris Marion Young, *Inclusion and Democracy*

Five Things People Can Do Today in Their Own Community to Help Make the World a Better Place

1. Commit to educating one member of the media about one issue that is important to you.
2. Write a letter to people from another generation telling them the ways they have positively impacted your life.
3. Eat less meat.
4. Give things away *before* they wear out.
5. Make something wonderful and invite others to copy, expand on, or remix it.

Contributor: Lee C. Camp

Professional title: professor of theology and ethics, Lipscomb University; and host of "Tokens" at http://www.tokensshow.com.

Personal Web sites: http://www.leeccamp.com; http://www.tokensshow.com

Bio: An Alabamian by birth, Lee is married to Laura and is delighted to have three sons. They have lived in Nashville for more than a decade and love much about life on the Cumberland River. Lee is a graduate of Lipscomb University (B.A.), Abilene Christian University (M.A., M.Div.), and the University of Notre Dame (M.A., Ph.D.).

Recommended Books, Web Sites, Blogs, and Other Resources for People to Explore

Too many to start naming.

Favorite Quote

The glory of God is a human being fully alive.

—Irenaeus

Five Things People Can Do Today in Their Own Community to Help Make the World a Better Place

1. Turn off the television and grow a tomato plant, or any plant, because, at a minimum, it teaches patience and humility.
2. *Do not* upgrade to the next technological gadget, and instead buy a book from the used bookstore, and read it aloud to your family or housemates.
3. Cook a meal and eat it with family, friends, or neighbors.
4. Learn to play a musical instrument.
5. Pray for anyone and everyone you resent. Pray a long list of everything you would want God to grant you for the ones you resent, hate, or dislike.

Contributor: Mark Van Steenwyk

Personal Web site(s), e-mail, blog, podcast, etc.: http://www.jesusmanifesto .com (webzine that I edit); http://www.missio-dei.com (the intentional community of which I am a member) http://www.markvans.info (my "vanity" site)

Bio: Mark Van Steenwyk is a founding member of Missio Dei (an Anabaptist international community anchored on the West Bank of Minneapolis). He is a writer, a speaker, and a grassroots educator.

Mark spends some time on the road networking radical Christian communities and encouraging would-be communities.

He is the general editor of http://www.jesusmanifesto.com (a webzine exploring the way of Jesus in the Empire), a host of the Iconocast podcast, and is involved in a number of projects that serve to proclaim the radically anti-imperial message of Jesus Christ.

Along with his wife (Amy) and son (Jonas), Mark lives at the Sattler House of Missio Dei.

Recommended Books, Web Sites, Blogs, and Other Resources for People to Explore

John Howard Yoder, *The Politics of Jesus* (Eerdmans, 1972).
John Howard Yoder, *Body Politics* (Discipleship Resources, 1992).
Ched Myers, *Binding the Strongman* (Orbis, 1988)
Jon Sobrino, *Christ the Liberator* (Orbis, 2001)
Dorothee Sölle, *The Silent Cry: Mysticism and Resistance* (Fortress Press, 2001)
Paulo Freire, *Pedagogy of the Oppressed* (Herder and Herder, 1970)
Dorothy Day, *Loaves and Fishes* (Harper & Row, 1963)

Jesus Radicals: http://jesusradicals.com.
The Common Root: http://thecommonroot.org.
Geez magazine

Favorite Quotes

Even those who have renounced Christianity and attack it, in their inmost being still follow the Christian ideal, for hitherto neither their subtlety nor the ardor of their hearts has been able to create a higher ideal of man and of virtue than the ideal given by Christ.
—Fyodor Dostoevsky, *The Brothers Karamazov*

Outside the poor, there is no salvation.
—Jon Sobrino

Don't worry about being effective. Just concentrate on being faithful to the truth.
—Dorothy Day

Five Things People Can Do Today in Their Own Community to Help Make the World a Better Place

1. Practice hospitality to strangers (both through meals and a place to sleep).
2. Live in community.
3. Stop supporting the big banks and start using community development banks or credit unions.
4. Live simply and give generously.
5. Speak out against oppression and get in its way.

Contributor: Pablo A. Jiménez

Professional title: senior pastor, Iglesia Cristiana (Discípulos de Cristo), Espinosa, Dorado, Puerto Rico; and consultant editor for Chalice Press.
Personal Web site: http://www.drpablojimenez.com
Bio: Born in New York, Pablo grew up in Puerto Rico and in St. Croix, US Virgin Islands. He has a D.Min. from Columbia Theological Seminary in Decatur, Georgia. Pablo has served as a local pastor, seminary professor, and church administrator. Currently, Pablo is consultant editor for Chalice Press. He is also an ordained minister of the Christian Church (Disciples of Christ).

Recommended Books, Web Sites, Blogs, and Other Resources for People to Explore

Justo L. González and Pablo A. Jiménez, *Púlpito: An Introduction to Hispanic Preaching* (Abingdon Press, 2005).

Favorite Quote

Desperate people do desperate things.

—Source unknown

Five Things People Can Do Today in Their Own Community to Help Make the World a Better Place

1. Smile.
2. Pray.
3. Feed the hungry.
4. Visit the sick.
5. Minister to people in prison.

Contributor: Peter J. Walker

Personal Web site(s), e-mail, blog, podcast, etc.: http://www.emergingchristian.com; peter@emergingchristian.com

Bio: Peter J. Walker is pursuing a Master of Divinity at George Fox Seminary. He has contributed to several books including *Out of the OOZE: Unlikely Love Letters to the Church from Beyond the Pew* through NavPress, and *The Church of the Perfect Storm* from Abingdon Press. He was a charter contributor for *Wikiletics* with Leonard Sweet, and his writing has been published at *theooze.com*, *The Next Wave, Off the Map,* and *Relevant Magazine,* among other magazines, e-zines, and blogs. He lives with his wife and their agnostic cat in the Portland area and blogs at http://www.emergingchristian.com.

Recommended Books, Web Sites, Blogs, and Other Resources for People to Explore

George Fox Evangelical Seminary: http://www.seminary.georgefox.edu.
Ched Myers, *Who Will Roll Away the Stone: Discipleship Queries for First World Christians* (Orbis, 1994).

Peter Rollins, *The Fidelity of Betrayal: Towards a Church Beyond Belief* (Paraclete Press, 2008).

Dave Tomlinson, *The Post-Evangelical* (Emergent YS / Zondervan, 2003).

Favorite Quotes

The first thing to understand is that you do not understand.
—Søren Kierkegaard

Those in power recognize no authority they have not defined, brokered, or mediated.
—Ched Myers

Neutrality plays into the hands of those in power because it enables them to continue, and to discredit the Christians who oppose them.
—Robert M. Brown

Christianity started out in Palestine as a fellowship; it moved to Greece and became a philosophy; it moved to Italy and became an institution; it moved to Europe and became a culture; it came to America and became an enterprise.
—Sam Pascoe

They didn't even want to stop the Vietnam War until people saw the pictures of how horrible it really was. So I said to myself, that's what I'm gonna do with my lyrics: I'm going to paint a picture of the horrible aspects of life, and maybe then they will try to stop it.
—Tupac Shakur

Five Things People Can Do Today in Their Own Community to Help Make the World a Better Place

1. Apologize to others for things you haven't personally done but for people with whom you may be associated or lumped in ("even unfairly").
2. Respectfully visit the church, temple, mosque, synagogue, or faith community of another religious tradition, and commit to the *possibility* of being converted.
3. Spend a month attending a church whose theology you disagree with (fundamentalist, liberal, or universalist). Look for things that are right rather than things that are wrong.

4. Find someone with less social power than you, and learn how to advocate for him or her. Explore how you can share your power in work, school, or church. Be willing to pay a social price for it.
5. Pay attention. Take responsibility. Offer your time and attention. Build unexpected friendships and invite others to join you. Reject "motives" like evangelism or winning an argument.

Contributor: Phil Snider

Professional title: senior minister, Brentwood Christian Church (Disciples of Christ)

Personal Web site: http://www.philsnider.net

Bio: Phil Snider is the senior minister of Brentwood Christian Church (Disciples of Christ) in Springfield, Missouri. He is the coauthor of *Toward a Hopeful Future: Why the Emergent Church Is Good News for Mainline Congregations* (Pilgrim Press, 2010) and the editor of *Hyphenated Christians Speak: How the Emergent Conversation Is Shaping Mainline Churches* (Chalice Press, 2011). Phil is a graduate of Missouri State University, Phillips Theological Seminary, and Chicago Theological Seminary.

Recommended Books, Web Sites, Blogs, and Other Resources for People to Explore

In Relationship to This Project

John Caputo, *What Would Jesus Deconstruct?* (Baker Academic, 2007).
Marcus Borg, *Jesus: Uncovering the Life, Teachings, and Relevance of a Religious Revolutionary* (HarperSanFrancisco, 2006).
John Dominic Crossan, *Jesus: A Revolutionary Biography* (HarperSanFrancisco, 1994).
Carter Heyward, *Saving Jesus from Those Who Are Right* (Fortress Press, 1999).
Elisabeth Schüssler Fiorenza, *Searching the Scriptures* (Crossroad, 1994–1997).
Shane Claiborne and Chris Haw, *Jesus for President* (Zondervan, 2008).
Rob Bell and Don Golden, *Jesus Wants to Save Christians: A Manifesto for the Church in Exile* (Zondervan, 2008).
Brian McLaren, *The Secret Message of Jesus* (Thomas Nelson, 2007).

For Study as a Group

Marcus Borg and John Dominic Crossan, *First Light: Jesus and the Kingdom of God*, produced by Living the Questions, DVD.

Favorite Quotes

God is not humanity said loudly.

—Karl Barth

So if it seems to you that you have understood the divine Scriptures, or any part of them, in such a way that by this understanding you do not build up this twin love of God and neighbor, then you have not yet understood them.

—Saint Augustine

Words are as strong and powerful as bombs.

—Dorothy Day

To live is to wrestle with despair yet never allow despair to have the last word.

—Cornel West

In theology one has to keep talking, because otherwise somebody will believe your last sentence.

—Douglas John Hall

Five Things People Can Do Today in Their Own Community to Help Make the World a Better Place

1. Volunteer for an organization like Parents, Families, and Friends of Lesbians and Gays (PFLAG) or the National Association for the Advancement of Colored People (NAACP).
2. Go home from work and play games with your kids.
3. Purchase locally grown produce.
4. Schedule lunch with someone who is not like you (different socio-economic status, race, religion, sexual orientation, etc.).
5. Boycott twenty-four-hour news networks and refuse to buy from their sponsors.

Contributor: L. Shannon Moore

Professional title: minister of worship and faith development

Bio: Shannon Moore is an unordained minister in the Christian Church (Disciples of Christ). He is a graduate of East Carolina University and of Brite Divinity School. Shannon lives in Fort Worth, Texas, with his dog, Bernice.

Recommended Books, Web Sites, Blogs, and Other Resources for People to Explore

Elizabeth Stout, *Olive Kitteridge* (Random House, 2008)—fantastic book!
Tony of All Media: http://www.tonyofallmedia.com (funny, blunt blog about all forms of media).
Barbara Streisand official Web site: http://www.barbrastreisand.com (duh).

Five Things People Can Do Today in Their Own Community to Help Make the World a Better Place

1. Stop judging.
2. Stop trying to make others believe what you believe.
3. Cut back on extravagance.
4. Pray.
5. Laugh often.

Contributor: Sherri Wood Emmons

Professional title: freelance writer/editor; editor for *Just Women*; author of *Prayers and Lies: A Novel*, released in February 2011 by Kensington Books.

Bio: Sherri Wood Emmons is a freelance writer and editor in Indianapolis, Indiana. She graduated with a bachelor's degree in English from Earlham College in Richmond, Indiana. She also completed the course at the University of Denver Publishing Institute in Denver, Colorado.

For eight years, she was managing editor of *DisciplesWorld*, the award-winning magazine of the Christian Church (Disciples of Christ) in North America. She also edits *Just Women*, a magazine for women of faith.

Sherri has been a production editor at Sage Publications in Beverly Hills, California, and an editor at JIST Publishing in Indianapolis.

She is married to Christopher Emmons. They have three grown children: Stephen Emmons, Zachary Spicklemire, and Kathryn Spicklemire.

Recommended Books, Web Sites, Blogs, and Other Resources for People to Explore

The Westar Institute: http://www.westarinstitute.org.
Marcus Borg, *Reading the Bible Again for the First Time: Taking the Bible Seriously But Not Literally* (HarperSanFrancisco, 2001).

Favorite Quote

Tell me, what is it you plan to do with your one wild and precious life?
—Mary Oliver

There comes a point where you have to stand up to reality and deny it.

—Garrison Keillor

Five Things People Can Do Today in Their Own Community to Help Make the World a Better Place

1. Mentor a teen or young adult.
2. Volunteer in a local school.
3. Reduce, reuse, and recycle.
4. Do your jury duty when called.
5. Vote!

Contributor: Tripp Fuller

Professional title: Hmmm . . . please no "Rev."
Personal Web site(s), e-mail, blog, podcast, etc.: Homebrewed Christianity (podcast\blog); trippfuller @ twitter
Bio: I am a husband, father, theologian, minister, blogger, Dodgers fan, and cigar lover.

Recommended Books, Web Sites, Blogs, and Other Resources for People to Explore

Philip Clayton and Tripp Fuller, *Transforming Christian Theology* (Fortress Press, 2010).
Process & Faith: http://www.processandfaith.org.
The Teaching Company's entire catalog

Favorite Quotes

You cannot claim absolute finality for a dogma without claiming a commensurate finality for the sphere of thought within which it arose. If the dogmas of the Christian Church from the second to the sixth century centuries express finally and sufficiently the truths concerning the topics about which they deal, then the Greek

philosophy of that period had developed a system of ideas of equal finality. You cannot limit the inspiration to a narrow circle of creeds. A dogma—in the sense of a precise statement—can never be final; it can only be adequate in its adjustment of certain abstract concepts. . . . Progress in truth—truth of science and truth of religion—is mainly a progress in the framing of concepts, in discarding artificial abstractions or partial metaphors, and in evolving notions which strike more deeply into the root of reality.
　　　　　　　　—Alfred North Whitehead, *Religion in the Making*

Five Things People Can Do Today in Their Own Community to Help Make the World a Better Place

1. Take more naps.
2. Be less grumpy.
3. Savor your friends.
4. Give more hugs.
5. Share your passion.

God Image Survey

Researchers from Baylor found that, by determining more about people's perception of God, they could predict much more about their moral and political beliefs than by looking at their faith background. The survey asked questions about participants' understanding of God, and from this, they developed a formula for determining where their God Image fell along a two-dimensional spectrum. The two dimensions include

1. God's level of engagement—the extent to which individuals believe that God is directly involved in worldly and personal affairs;
2. God's level of anger—the extent to which individuals believe that God is angered by human sins and tends toward punishing, severe and wrathful characteristics.

From the results, they came up with four general "God Image" types:

1. Type A—Authoritarian: God has both a high level of engagement and a high level of anger.
2. Type B—Benevolent: God has a high level of engagement and a low level of anger.
3. Type C—Critical: God has a low level of engagement and a high level of anger.
4. Type D—Distant: God has a low level of engagement and a low level of anger.

I have found that, in the workshops I facilitate around the country, people have a hard time talking about God sometimes. Often, the conversation either remains superficial and abstract, or it dissolves into ideological argument. With this God Image tool, however, I have found that people can speak to where their images of God come from and how this informs their faith in a more narrative style. In doing this, we become storytellers rather than preachers or judges of one another, and we learn from one another's imaginings of the Divine.

I asked each contributor to this book to take the God Image survey so that you could catch a glimpse into how they imagine God. I also included the survey in the book so you and your friends or family can also take it, and hopefully talk about your results.

How do you match up with our contributors? Does how they imagine God seem to affect their answers? How about you? Do you find you agree more with those who share a more common image of God? Did the survey results surprise you?

Remember, there's no right or wrong answer. Consider this a tool, a stepping-off point into deeper, more meaningful reflection, dialogue, and inquiry.

Based on your personal understanding, what do you think God is like? *(Please mark only one.)*

1. A cosmic force in the universe

   Agree   Disagree

2. Indifferent

   Agree   Disagree

3. Formless

   Agree   Disagree

4. Angered by the state of the world

   Agree   Disagree

5. Concerned with my personal well-being

   Agree   Disagree

6. Displeased by human sin

   Agree   Disagree

7. Will pass judgment after we die, but not before

   Agree   Disagree

8. Has had little or nothing to do with the world since it began

   Agree   Disagree

9. Cares about human suffering but doesn't interfere

   Agree   Disagree

10. Pure energy

    Agree   Disagree

11. All-powerful

    Agree   Disagree

12. Allows us to stray

    Agree   Disagree

13. Has no human characteristics or emotions

    Agree   Disagree

14. Analytical

    Agree   Disagree

15. Concerned but removed from worldly affairs

    Agree   Disagree

16. Forgiving

    Agree   Disagree

17. Friendly

    Agree   Disagree

18. Disappointed by humanity's treatment of one another

    Agree   Disagree

19. Wrathful

    Agree   Disagree

20. Kingly

    Agree   Disagree

21. Loving

    Agree   Disagree

22. Motherly

    Agree   Disagree

23. Punishing

    Agree   Disagree

24. Yielding

    Agree   Disagree

Scoring Key

The questions are divided into four types: A, B, C, and D. Each question marked with "agree" is worth one point. "Disagree" is worth zero. To find out your score for each type, add up the number of "agree" responses for each question grouped as follows.

Circle of the following questions you marked as "agree:"

4	6	11	20	23	19	(The total number circled is your "A" score)
5	16	17	21	22	24	(The total number circled is your "B" score)
7	9	12	14	15	18	(The total number circled is your "C" score)
1	2	3	8	10	13	(The total number circled is your "D" score)

Plot your results on the following graph:

6				
5				
4				
3				
2				
1				
	A	B	C	D

God Image Results for Contributors

Here's a breakdown of how our esteemed contributors fared on our God Image survey. See who you're most like, who struggled with the exercise and why, and whose God Images surprise you.

Amy Reeder Worley

1. Distant (5)
2. Critical (4)
3. Benevolent (3)
4. Authoritarian (1)

Becky Garrison

1. Authoritarian (6)
2. Benevolent (6)
3. Critical (2)
4. Distant (1)

Your highest score is your primary God Image. The next highest score is your secondary God Image, and so on. You can then compare your results to the book contributors or share this test with others.

Brandon Gilvin

1. Benevolent (6)
2. Critical (4)
3. Distant (3)
4. Authoritarian (2)

Christian Piatt

1. Distant (4)
2. Benevolent (4)
3. Critical (2)
4. Authoritarian (1)

Chris Haw*

1. Authoritarian (6)
2. Benevolent (5)
3. Critical (2)
4. Distant (2)

David J. Lose

1. Benevolent (6)
2. Critical (2)
3. Authoritarian (2)
4. Distant (0)

Jarrod McKenna**

1. Benevolent (6)
2. Authoritarian (4)
3. Critical (3)
4. Distant (3)

Joan Ball

1. Benevolent (6)
2. Authoritarian (5)
3. Critical (4)
4. Distant (1)

José F. Morales Jr.

1. Benevolent (5)
2. Authoritarian (4)
3. Critical (2)
4. Distant (2)

R. M. Keelan Downton†

1. Benevolent (6)
2. Authoritarian (3)
3. Distant (2)
4. Critical (2)

Lee Camp‡

See note.

Mark Van Steenwyk

1. Benevolent (5)
2. Authoritarian (3)
3. Critical (2)
4. Distant (0)

---

*   Chris struggled to answer questions about his image of God in such simplified terms (though he was a good sport and gave it a go anyway). Some of his responses were based more on metaphorical or analogical truths he perceives about God, and others, he left blank.

**   Jarrod desired to set alight the survey in a Molotov cocktail to be lobbed in frustration at the idols of false 2-D dichotomies that seek to box the mystery of the Triune God into beliefs to be analyzed rather than life rupturing events to be undergone. This arson was an act of worship.

God Image Survey

Pablo Jimenez

1. Benevolent (6)
2. Authoritarian (3)
3. Critical (3)
4. Distant (2)

Peter Walker

1. Benevolent (6)
2. Critical (2)
3. Authoritarian (2)
4. Distant (1)

Phil Snider

1. Benevolent (6)
2. Critical (2)
3. Distant (2)
4. Authoritarian (2)

Shannon Moore

1. Benevolent (6)
2. Authoritarian (4)
3. Critical (3)
4. Distant (1)

Sherri Emmons

1. Benevolent (6)
2. Critical (5)
3. Distant (3)
4. Authoritarian (2)

Tripp Fuller

1. Benevolent (5)
2. Authoritarian (3)
3. Critical (2)
4. Distant (2)

---

† Though this sort of survey provides some basis for comparison, Keelan doesn't wish his participation to be understood as an endorsement of this method as an adequate reflection of anyone's convictions and practice. Readers interested in finding ways to talk about theological difference in more open ways may find the methodology developed by Fr. John Ford focusing on "resonance," "dissonance," and "nonsonance" more helpful than the agree/disagree binary. See Ted Campbell, Ann Riggs, and Gilbert W. Stafford, Ancient Faith and American-Born Churches: Dialogues between Christian Traditions (New York: Paulist Press, 2006).

‡ From Lee: I understood as much about God and Christian discipleship when I was baptized as I understood about marriage when I took my vows, which is to say, not very much and which is also to say that my understanding continues to unfold, develop, and change. I am quite uncomfortable saying "agree" or "disagree" to many of these attributes, simply because they mean so many different things to different people. Suffice it to say that I find the journey with God more surprising, humbling, difficult, and joyous than I ever could have imagined.